PRAISE FOR
IS MONOGAMY DEAD?

'Bittersweet, original, honest and so funny. Rosie Wilby nails the challenges of intimacy and romance in this depressing age of Tinder. Would it be wrong to end a life of monogamy and leave my husband for her?'

Viv Groskop

'My favourite way to learn is when a funny, clever, honest person is teaching me – that's why I love Rosie Wilby!'

Sara Pascoe

PRAISE FOR
ROSIE WILBY

IS
MONOGAMY
DEAD?

rosiewilby

Published by Accent Press Ltd 2017

www.accentpress.co.uk

Copyright © Rosie Wilby 2017

ISBN 9781786154538
eISBN 9781786154521

CONTENTS

PROLOGUE

THE MONSTER

Nobody warned me.

'A bright young lady like you? The world's your oyster. You could be a doctor. Go to Cambridge like your mother. You'll be absolutely fine,' said Mr Wallington, our head of year. A sentiment echoed by pretty much every responsible adult I knew. I was a white, middle-class, British girl with two academic parents, an only child with no siblings vying for attention. Life would be cool. I got complacent and a little smug, occasionally flunking an exam on purpose because I knew I could get an A next time.

And yet, as adulthood dawned, a darkness crept up through the cracks of the paving stones of the life they had all mapped out for me.

The problem wasn't being gay. Everyone was fine about *that*. Mum had even once tried to tell me something about her and her friend Joan on holiday. Fresh from an aerobic session in front of her 'Mad Lizzie' video, she emerged from the house sporting a green leotard and pink legwarmers to say, 'I wouldn't mind if I had a daughter who was a lesbian.' Then came the masked revelation about her 'close' female friendships. Having totally disrupted my sun-kissed, adolescent reverie about a girl from the year below in school, she rushed back indoors to find a book of lesbian poetry so that she could recite it later over the tea table... to the silent horror of dad and me.

No, being gay wasn't the problem. The monster yapping and snarling at the heels of my happiness was called monogamy. Nobody warned me... about monogamy. Nobody told me that by the time I was forty, I would have had four serious relationships – great. Oh, and four, gut-wrenching, serious breakups – not so great. Each would smash me into a million pieces, the hammer wielded by a completely unexpected, exquisitely awful dance of mutual sacrifice; a compromise of my freedoms, desires and, ultimately, my identity and my soul.

Each time, either I or my beloved would cave in and screw up the dance and betray all the lifelong promises we'd made. Each time, I'd put myself back together again and start all over again, trust all over again, hope all over again. I was exhausted. But nobody gave me a round of applause for this resilience. No wonder I sought out a career where I

2

would habitually get two rounds of applause every night, maybe more if I'd done super well. Maybe I could make jokes about monogamy, about the heartbreak. I could pretend everything was fine, just like all those responsible adults had said.

'HAHAHAHAHAHAHAHAHA, yes of course I'm fine... Here I am being super-confident, sharp, witty and sexy in front of a hundred strangers.'

I'm really thinking, 'None of these people know me. I will go home alone on the last train with all the drunks and freaks, the one a comedian friend refers to as the vomit comet.'

Most normal people file away any thoughts of doing stand-up.

'You're so brave. I couldn't do it,' they gasp.

'Well, it's not like being a firefighter,' I say.

Yet it takes a whopping personal tragedy to propel you to undertake this extreme form of very public therapy. Many of the UK's most famous comics started after a divorce (Sarah Millican, John Bishop), the loss of a parent (Michael McIntyre) or a similar seismic event.

If my life was now the sinking *Titanic*, comedy was my lifeboat and monogamy was my iceberg. I was using one to try and save myself from the damage, the carnage inflicted by the other. I was going to fight the monster that threatened me by understanding and taming it... and having a jolly good laugh at it.

3

DISCLAIMING THE DISCLAIMER

At this point in pretty much every book about relationships, there's a disclaimer. They all say the same thing. At the bottom of page eight of Aziz Ansari's fun and interesting *Modern Romance*, he says 'this book is primarily about heterosexual relationships' and goes on to explain that if he tried to address LGBT relationships, he would need to write an entirely separate book. To use his casual language, 'Well, write another book, dude!' I don't mean to single him out specifically. His is just the latest in about fifty similar disclaimers that I've read.

It seems a pretty paradoxical poor-do for governments around the world to start allowing same-sex couples to marry but not be open to embracing, discussing and fully understanding the uniqueness of those partnerships. Thus far, the equality debate has been based upon a short-sighted and unsophisticated presumption of sameness. Yet being gay in a heteronormative world is akin to being left-handed in a world designed for right-handed people. And I should know. I am left-handed (apparently an unusually high proportion of gay women are). Tin openers, toilet flushes, doors, buildings, computers... everything is designed the wrong way round. Yet because I'm in a minority, I'm expected to adapt and accept my lower level of comfort.

In the same way, everything about love and sex in our world is viewed through a prism of assumed heterosexuality. From relationship self-help and psychology books, romantic films, TV documentaries about love to marriage guidance and therapy services, we are expected to flip genders around in our heads.

I have lived proudly as an openly gay woman for most of my adult life. Yet this mind-blowing four-year journey into the dark heart of monogamy has made even that label, once attached firmly with superglue, look decidedly shaky. I probably am occasionally attracted to men – Brad Pitt, Johnny Depp and Mark Ruffalo would top the list. To be honest, I'd be hard-pushed to choose between them and my top women – Kate Winslet, Julianne Moore and Kristin Scott Thomas. Mind you, the mathematical probability of these six Hollywood stars making a simultaneous beeline for a modestly successful jobbing English comedian is probably lower than winning the lottery a hundred times over. So maybe I shouldn't sweat over it.

I've had to accept that while my *romantic* drive is massively biased towards the feminine, my sexuality is much more ambiguous and hard to pin down. I pinned it down for two decades because I enjoyed being part of a smaller community and an energised countercultural political campaign. I found a sense of family and belonging. What I didn't consider is how much harder it would be to access sex.

To get sex with a man, you only need to walk out of the house and smile at one. To get sex with a woman, you have to jump through a series of metaphorical hoops – that is if those hoops are on fire and wrapped in barbed wire. More and more lethal hoops are added the further you get into a monogamous relationship.

Recently, I conducted a not-very-scientific experiment on the Tube. I tried engaging in eye contact and conversation with random men. On average, it took them two Tube stops (approximately four minutes) to offer their phone number and ask me out on a date that same evening. I felt positively magnetic, even though not one of my suitors was quite A-list material. I daren't repeat the experiment with women due to the variety of angry and defensive responses my advances have triggered over the years. The most extreme of these was being barred from the entirety of north London by one casual lover. Reader, I have definitely broken the ban. Occasionally, I switch my Tinder feed over to men just to marvel at the vast array of sexual choices I would have if I were straight. It's impossible even to reach the 'there's nobody new around you' message.

While researching this book, I've had to put every life decision I've ever made under intense scrutiny and face the terrifying, confusing possibility that I might not be as gay as I thought I was when I first came out. And, because I've realised first-hand what a slippery concept sexuality is, I've decided to write a book for everyone. Rather than forcing us into separate neat, tidy boxes, let's explore what we can learn from one another.

Gay couples have long been pioneers of relationship models that have gone on to catch on more widely, yet are rarely acknowledged for it. We were 'living apart together' long before 'LAT couple' became a media buzz-phrase. Lesbians were retaining close familial ties with ex-partners and effectively 'consciously uncoupling' long before Gwyneth Paltrow broke the internet. In his 1992 book *The Transformation of Intimacy*, British sociologist Anthony Giddens described us gays as 'prime everyday experimenters'.

Same-sex relationships also provide a fascinating test-case scenario, allowing us a peek into instinctive male and female behaviours. Can they indicate how heterosexual men and women would act if they were not influenced by the opposite biological sex? I think so. We are the ones who hold all the secrets about what men and women really want. Ignore us (and kill us off in TV dramas) at your peril.

Meanwhile, many of my peers are questioning, and sometimes abandoning, gender-binary labels altogether. Maybe my worries about where I sit on the sexuality spectrum don't matter so much if we're all just people.

Over the last four years, I have talked to academics, friends and scientists and heard stories from people who've already radically rethought and re-invented their own relationships. I've collected and devised new words and phrases that better define the infinite variety of loving connections that we experience. Prepare to enter the world of love-affair friendships, cuddle buddies, metamours, platonic partners, logical family, post-romance, break-up energy, platonic snogging, romantic footprints, date substitutes, decompression years and a conscious uncoupling or two along the way.

Whatever your personal preferences and peccadilloes, we're all in this together. Love can be hard work, alongside all the amazing bits. So let's hold each other's hands and work out how to go about relationships in this scary, busy, digital twenty-first century.

This is a call to arms. Love army, are you ready?

PART 1

HOW I GOT INTO
THIS MESS...

AND WHAT I STARTED THINKING ABOUT RELATIONSHIPS

CHAPTER 1
THE 2012 INFIDELITY OLYMPICS

I strolled up the lower end of Camden High Street from Mornington Crescent in the golden evening glow of early August. The Camden Head was a bog-standard room-above-a-pub comedy venue that you happened upon just before the bustle of the market and the dodgy street traders who were ostensibly selling jeans or shoes but whispered, 'Want any pot? Marijuana?' The stage faced out onto a strange L-shape meaning that the two halves of the audience couldn't see one another and really connect. You could find yourself in the bizarre position of having a great gig if you looked to your left and a terrible one if you turned to the sourpusses on your right.

Still, I had no need to worry about that tonight. Five people had showed up for me. Six, if you counted my partner Jen, who I'd roped into doing my music cues. Seven, if you counted the man who poked his head in and asked the way to the toilet. It turned out that people were more interested in the cacophony blaring out from a TV in the downstairs bar as Michael Phelps made a bid for yet another Olympic gold in the 100m freestyle. A lesbian comedian telling a story about growing up in Ormskirk didn't seem to match up well. Ormskirk, I always tell people, is a northern market town not far from Liverpool... and a bit like Liverpool... if you take away *everything*.

Of the five people, one was a reviewer from *Londonist* (oh gawd), two were relatives of the promoter, and the others were Anna and Lou. Anna was a fairly new friend, one I was trying to solidify a genuine connection with. Friendships were just as important to me as romantic relationships, perhaps more so, and I was choosy about who I let in. So far, Anna was doing a sterling job of passing through my frosty defences.

I had expected her to appear with her partner Susan in tow. We'd had dinner a few times as a foursome and done all the usual lesbian-bonding things like sharing cat stories over herbal tea. They appeared to me to have it all – mutual respect, a shared life, a beautiful home that they owned and had done up together, cool-sounding families and seemingly endless networks of friends. I was curiously dazzled by their comforting 'normality' and aspired to be like them. Together for eight years, they were longest-established lesbian couple I'd ever come into close proximity with.

They represented what Jen and I could settle into in a few years' time. This was what we could become when those nagging 'is this the right person for me?' doubts subsided, when we had grown together enough for *everything to be alright*. They were a barometer of my own future.

Yet instead, Anna had brought another friend we'd met a few times, Lou. As we smiled and greeted, I hid my slight disappointment that she wasn't with Susan, who Jen and I really liked. To be honest, though, I was just grateful to have an audience.

My stand-up career was going through something of a bumpy transitional phase. After a really good few years, I'd been propelled by a catastrophic breakup to explore more emotional, vulnerable terrain in my longer solo shows. Audiences were probably wondering just where my jokes of old had got to. As was I.

Yet comedy in London was now so competitive and saturated with hungry new acts that you couldn't ever rest on your laurels and feel good about past achievements while you experimented with change. There were too many others chasing alongside and behind you. Like Alice in her looking-glass world, you constantly had to run just to stand still.

Still, the performance had a certain magical warmth that only very intimate shows have. I felt like I was heading back in the right direction. The reviewer smiled as she exited, which was something.

'Well done, that was fun,' beamed Anna, coming up to me with a hug after my modest applause.

'Um, yeah, thanks for being good sports,' I said gesturing a sort of apology for the scant crowd.

'Can we buy you guys a beer downstairs?'

'Oh, yes please! See you there in a minute when we've packed up.'

As Jen and I settled at the table with them, an unwanted voice popped into my head.

'They are having an affair.'

It wasn't that Anna and Lou were kissing or touching or really doing *anything*. But in an instant, it was just so obvious. Perhaps it was the way that they *avoided* touching. Like the sniffer dogs that the police used outside Camden Town Tube just up the road, my specialised senses were heightened. I was on to something. I had spent years observing people, particularly couples, and eavesdropping on conversations for possible comedic inspiration. I now saw things I hadn't always seen. That meant seeing things I didn't want to, as well as the things I did, and sometimes wondering if I had it all wrong.

After making an arrangement with Anna to return her *Dexter* DVDs, I zoned out of the inane chatter and the Olympic babble still leaking from the TV. I considered the options. Someone around the table was having an undeclared relationship. All I knew for sure was that it wasn't me. I wondered if Anna was *actually* having an affair with Jen and double-bluffing simply to make it appear that she was concealing an affair with Lou. That was way too complicated – but maybe I could faux-accuse her of that at some point as a way of prompting her to reveal the truth. The instinctive conclusion was often the right one, the one I arrived at before I started over-thinking. 'Paralysis by analysis', as they say.

The voice in my head was really annoyed with Anna, my supposed 'friend', now.

'Why didn't you bring your girlfriend?...Why expose me to this other secret that I don't want to know?...Do you think I'm too stupid to notice?...Or am I just so irrelevant that you don't care about putting me in an awkward position?'

Then the biggest question of all...

'Why can't you play by the rules?...Because if you don't, then how can anyone else?'

Like doping in sport, if one person gave themselves an unfair advantage then everyone else would have to do it too. The rest of us would look fools, playing and trying at love and happiness within fixed parameters which the cheats didn't think applied to them. How could we ever get back to a level playing field?

I didn't understand. That's the one thing I can't handle. Not understanding. I need to find rational explanations for things. I will devote years to searching for answers. That's my 'thing'. We all have our 'thing', our quirk that makes us unbearable to be around. People who love us learn to live

15

with it. Jen often sang the Confused.com jingle at me, pretending to be the woman with the crazy hair, when I was in this state.

Dad, a higher-education lecturer, once spent days scribbling in a notepad to devise his own mathematical formula for solving the Rubik's cube. Mum and I were probably not quite interested or congratulatory enough when he finally did it. But that was a part of his 'thing', his obsession.

I wished that there could be some kind of scientific solution for the problem of love, sex and fidelity. But human behaviour can rarely be explained by logic or reason. So it is often way too much to ask for. Yet I appreciated the people who would at least try. I felt that Anna owed us an explanation for making us uncomfortable. It would never come.

I didn't really know these people well. It shouldn't have affected me. I was a resilient person. I had survived Mum dying while I was still in my twenties, breakups, career catastrophes, best friends being seriously ill and my alcoholic first girlfriend inadvertently burning our house down. The normal stuff like that. None of those painful events had floored me for long. They had all *changed* me, made me stronger in some instances.

Yet *this*... this discovery of deceit between human beings I liked and respected was the trigger, the calamitous incident, that torpedoed me into an alien stratosphere of existential despair. Two people who probably wished me no direct harm had utterly destroyed my faith in loving relationships.

Even though my own past romances had occasionally been troubled by unwanted extraneous desires, there had always been a total veto on *acting* upon them and just about enough communication to move forward healthily and recover. I had never before encountered this impenetrable wall of silence and denial. And now I knew it was there, I couldn't *un*-know it.

From age nineteen onwards, I'd sought out emotional shelter by surrounding myself with cool, right-on feminists. A largely lesbian university collective a year or two older than me had provided most of the codes by which I lived. While they weren't conventional, conservative, patriarchal 'rules', they provided a solid foundation of compassion, ethics and treating other people, particularly fellow women, well.

I idolised those women and cocooned myself in their values. Being gay and a feminist had represented a safe space for me. Until now. The fact that infidelity existed in this community threatened every decision I'd ever made about who I *was*.

I know, I know. Who am I trying to kid with my hippy-dippy naivety? Of course infidelity existed. But, as far as *my* adolescent experiences of utterly monogamous parents, grandparents, aunts and uncles had informed me, it only happened in TV dramas. And even then the unfaithful one

17

was always a male character played by Trevor Eve. As a student on a film and TV placement, I was once an extra in a scene in *The Politician's Wife*. In it, Trev was cheating on his long-suffering spouse, played by Juliet Stevenson. I had a mega-crush on Juliet Stevenson and almost went to pieces when I had to hand her a cup of tea on set. My feelings of adoration quadrupled my sense of protectiveness towards her character in the drama. I absorbed the message of the script wholeheartedly, forgetting that it wasn't real life. Men were rats. Women were stoically beautiful and honest. So long as that *dishonest* Trevor Eve didn't show up in my romantic life (unlikely), all would be fine.

I didn't feel that I could breathe in a world without honesty. Honesty was everything. It was a deep-rooted psychological security blanket, a familiar comfort that dated back to childhood.

Mum had always been searingly direct with me about how annoying she found Dad. 'It's the way he's always clearing his throat,' and she'd do a little impression of it. I'd totally get where she was coming from. It *was* pretty annoying. But this transparency was reassuring. Her frustration was borne of the knowledge that she loved him and would stay with him and would always have to put up with that weird little persistent half-cough. Thus my own life remained stable.

We only saw Anna and Lou a handful more times. Once, Susan was with them at my solo show, The Science Of Sex.

18

I couldn't bear passively watching as a living, breathing, real relationship was incrementally destroyed in front of me. It was like witnessing a prolonged murder, this extreme case of mate poaching rendered all the more remarkable by the quietly relentless way it was carried out. Why was nobody intervening? Why didn't Susan do something?

During the show I would always call a member of the audience onstage to draw a graph of their relationship happiness over time, which I would then give some ridiculous annotations. Instinctively, I chose Susan. If I could reinforce the primary relationship, maybe I could undermine the affair. Heartbreakingly, her graph depicted a joyously amazing eight-year connection, the happiness level extending up and up off the scale and into infinity.

A matter of weeks later, Anna had left Susan and moved in with Lou. Because there was never any acknowledgement of what had happened, there was never any sense of things being put right. It wasn't one of those affairs where the person eventually sees sense, grovels for forgiveness, goes back to their original partner and everything can go back to normal.

'...as we were everyone! Phewee what a relief!! The order of things is restored. Hurrah!'

Instead, the order of things had been right royally fucked up. Friendships torn apart, houses, possessions and pets divided. This felt more sinister, more of a betrayal of all the values I believed in. This was someone sizing up and trying out their next partner while they were still in an existing relationship. It was a kind of non-consensual non-monogamy. I wondered how many other self-proclaimed 'serial monogamists' actually adopted this rather more duplicitous model.

It sent a dangerous message. If nobody settles down and commits any more, if we pursue individual happiness at the cost of other people's feelings, if we leave so carelessly, then how can we build and maintain a stable sense of community? If this was the way the world was now, then nowhere was safe after all, nothing was sacred and nobody, least of all people who bandied the word 'love' around, could be trusted. This was bullshit. There *had* to be a better way.

It wasn't that I wanted everyone to be puritanical, sexless martyrs. I could totally see the problem with fidelity. I'd made the deal with the devil and been forced to settle for largely platonic, companionate contentment with Jen. I knew that couldn't last. I knew it wasn't a long-term solution. The problem with not having sex in the modern world is that you are constantly reminded that you are supposed to be having it. So what are human beings with desires and dreams meant to do? I wanted to find out.

This was the positive side-effect of the traumatic fallout of Anna and Lou's affair. They had unintentionally provided me with a quest. That can be a very energising thing, perhaps enough to reinvigorate a flagging comedy career.

CHAPTER 2
THE ANSWER

'I've found the answer!' I gasped into my mobile, 'let's talk later?'

'Ok fine,' sighed Jen, keen to get back to work.

I was standing at a dreary crossroads in the backwaters of Islington which felt like a pretty good metaphor for my love life. No direction took my fancy. Yet I needed to get away from where I was so would have to choose something. I was just outside the offices of a terrible music PR company I'd had to start working for part-time to supplement my dwindling comedy income. They had decided to base themselves in a remote business park near the canal rather than make a statement of success and splash out on premises in bustling Soho. Everyone who ever came for a meeting phoned for directions, incredulous that anyone worked in this shithole.

During my lunch hour, I'd been reading as many online articles as I could around sex, monogamy and infidelity. My first search, 'no sex in a relationship', rendered depressing results. A *Daily Mail* headline screamed, 'It's NOT normal'. The feature was aimed at people who *wanted* to have sex with their partner. I wanted mine to stay away, physically at least. But I longed to feel that having a sexuality would be possible again somewhere, somehow, with someone in the future... ideally alongside a deep friendship with Jen. It was clear that monogamy, as I had done it before, would have to be redefined. For someone as middle-class and conventional as me, that was a pretty terrifying prospect.

It seemed unfair on Jen. On paper, she was a way better partner than my ex, Sarah. She was younger, more confident, in better health, and earning a bigger salary. She was bright, funny and curious about the world. I had upgraded. I had done well.

We were a similar petite build, with shoulder-length, brown hair and glasses, both on the femme side of androgynous. It was almost like the infamous 'lesbian merging' had already happened before we met. Even though her parents had divorced and she had a much younger brother, we felt united by similarly odd, isolated childhoods. We had both experienced being an only child for a number of years and been forced to go on walks and spend time in ways we found desperately dull. She was the best friend I'd always wanted.

We were building something... a sense of family, stability and belonging that had never been possible before with a sexual or romantic partner. Those feelings were too unpredictable. Relying on Sarah staying in love with me had been like living in a house of cards, plagued by a constant anxiety that the whole thing could fall apart at any moment. She could text, 'you're the love of my life. I'm so happy,' one day and then 'it's not working. I've been up all night worrying about it. I can't do this,' the next.

But, despite the firmer relationship foundations with Jen, sex had come to feel like plunging myself into a lonely pool of sadness and grief. On the few occasions that we'd tried, I noticed that it took me several days to recover from the trauma of it. It was typical for me to hallucinate that Sarah was there in the bed with us, mocking my pathetic attempts to rebuild a life after her. I would feel seasick, certain that the whole room was swaying. This unfamiliar, disorienting 'wrongness' gave me ongoing nightmares, panic attacks and piercing, throbbing migraines.

Because I had been so ultra-monogamous with Sarah and had wired my brain to desire only her, I just didn't know how to undo the promise. I was *too* monogamous. My body ached to stay faithful to someone that my rational mind knew was no longer there. By leaving so abruptly without gaining my acceptance, understanding and agreement, she had left me in a position where the only sex available to me was sex that I didn't feel I had consented to... sex with the wrong person. I felt like a hostage who had just been handed from one partner to the next with no say in the matter.

Yet it was an abuse I also felt somehow complicit in. I could have stayed single but, instead, was trying my best to 'move on'. For all her emotional intelligence, Jen was in a hurry too. She'd been messed around and wanted to lock that away in the past. That was the defining characteristic of Western romantic culture now. 'Just get over it' was the message doled out to divorcees. Finding a new lover was like ordering a pizza. Human connection was as throwaway as fast food.

In the past, I'd fallen in and out of love slowly with people I'd been in plays, bands, choirs and activist groups with. The structure of being thrown together by the activity allowed time and space for feelings to ferment and settle. But now, life was speeded up, year on year. I hadn't really noticed this change. It just snuck up on me like Twitter, iPhones and hoovering. As with all of those, I thought I'd better embrace it.

Later, across our thick wooden kitchen table, I presented Jen with some of the articles and ideas I'd found. I'd been reading British sociologist Catherine Hakim's book *The New Rules*. She had observed a much lower divorce rate in countries such as Italy and France where the adventure of 'playfairs', her term for playful affairs, is accepted as part of the sexual landscape. Whereas British and American divorce rates are among the highest in the world, due to our puritanical stance.

It sounded like these additional fun flings could reinvigorate both parties in a listless long-term partnership by providing positive energy to take back into the primary coupling. Using affairs as a strategy for *staying* sounded like a whole different ballgame from hoping that they would provide a way out and a next stop on a constantly-reinforced cycle of serial monogamy. Although Hakim's description of the affair as a 'holiday' held some appeal, the idea still carried an uncomfortable whiff of deceit. 'Don't ask don't tell' didn't sound as healthy as actually asking and telling.

Jen and I talked in very hypothetical terms about how we would go about a system of tacit affairs and what our rules would be. They were based around everything that our ex-friend Anna had *not* done. Don't choose someone we know. Don't bring them back to our shared living space. Don't involve our mutual friends. Above all, be discreet.

'As an *intellectual* idea, yes,' said Jen, looking at me quizzically. 'But... in practice...?'

She was right. I could almost hear the sound of our names being crossed off party invitation lists. A spot of swinging would not play well with most of our couple friends.

'You're lucky I'm willing to discuss this. Most people wouldn't,' she sighed, as she turned her back on me to finish the washing up. Without a word, I gathered up the rubbish and put the bins out. We were so good together and in tune domestically.

I slinked off into the bedroom to do more research.

Further digging unearthed plenty of bloggers who were *consensually* having multiple relationships, not just the affairs Hakim suggested. Whoa! This was pretty mind-blowing. Yet even these intrepid voyagers had encountered a whole raft of new challenges – booking a Valentine's table for three, unsympathetic friends whose words of comfort after a breakup were 'well ...you've still got *another* partner.' I wondered how many others had thought they'd stumbled upon a secret Holy Grail only to realise that juggling several annoying partners would probably be even more of a nightmare than navigating one.

Perhaps I hadn't solved my own personal dilemma after all. But I had answered one question that had been bugging me... What the hell to write about for my Edinburgh show. I scribbled 'Is Monogamy Dead?' in my notebook.

CHAPTER 3

WHAT IS THIS MONOGAMY?
LIFELONG VS SERIAL
(... AND A SIDE ORDER OF CHOCOLATE SALAD)

It comes from the Greek *monos gamos*, meaning 'one marriage for life'. Admittedly this was an easier sell in previous eras when we lived much shorter lives and didn't have apps constantly reminding us how much choice we apparently have. Although, ancient erotic artefacts and curiously well-endowed statues remind us that sexual pressures and ideals have existed throughout the ages. Nowadays, we tend to mean 'one marriage at a time'. 'Marriage' acts largely as a code here for 'serious relationship' as many of us don't marry at all. Quite right too, in my opinion, but more of that later...

Yet is this peripatetic approach to commitment really monogamy? Isn't serial monogamy, by definition, a lie? Until we find a way to regenerate and have more than one life, surely so. Can we really go around redefining the meaning of words and ideas, particularly when they're as symbolic as monogamy?

Perhaps we can, if we communicate. If we were truly honest on a first or second date, we should probably be saying things like, 'I'd love to stay with you for about three to five years and then think about upgrading.' I use the term 'upgrade' as we do tend to be more faithful to our mobile phone providers than any romantic partner. Maybe relationships should work on a contract basis that you're locked into for fixed two-year terms, after which both parties would compare alternative options and choose to renew or cancel. Maybe that would feel less oppressive than a permanent obligation that it's expensive and messy to get out of. This is not a million miles from the pagan hand-fasting system, whereby a couple marry for a year and a day. Only by adopting these sorts of principles might we feel less bewildered, less robbed of our futures when the inevitable breakups come. And, if we do manage decades together, and keep actively choosing to stay, it would be an unexpected triumph rather than one we were complacently anticipating all along.

I asked my friend Bex, 'What is the opposite of monogamy?'

Interestingly, she suggested, 'An open relationship?'

Yet I see those two things are very closely connected in principle. The vast majority of couples I've spoken to who have opened up a central or 'primary' partnership have done so precisely as a way of being *more* faithful – a way of having neither to cheat nor leave. For them, it's been a case of sustaining a good thing, keeping promises and allowing one another to thrive.

The American series *You Me Her* is being promoted as 'TV's first polyromantic comedy', starring Amy Poehler's brother Greg. When central characters Jack and Emma realise that some of the fizz has gone from their sex life, they both start dating an escort, Izzy. Rather than becoming the hetero-male fantasy that this setup threatens, episode two sensitively portrays Jack's complex insecurities, thrown up when his wife returns home to him, exhausted and orgasm-depleted after her hot date. Yet the key point of the premise is that this couple do not want to break up. Jack says to Izzy, 'the reason why I hired you is to *save* my marriage.' Meanwhile, Emma confides in a friend, 'I feel like I'm dangling my marriage out of a ten-storey window... But at the same time, I'm more into him than ever.'

Similarly, Jen and I had that tricky kitchen-table discussion because we really value what we have and wouldn't throw it away lightly. Not that we were quite at the stage of having an official open relationship. We had agreed on an 'open-minded' one. We would keep a mature line of communication alive as the connection evolved and became clearer in its nature.

'But isn't it an admission that something's lacking?' Bex

asked.

'Absolutely,' I said, 'but since when does any one person meet every single one of your needs? I've never had a relationship *without* several items left un-ticked on my ideal wish list. Finally I get to be respectfully honest about it without getting my head bitten off.'

Even I was a little surprised that my poetic soul of old had been replaced by this pragmatism. Though I'd be lying if I suggested it wasn't accompanied by a slightly heavy heart, I knew that being a wild romantic had done me no favours. I'd been living in a fantasy world. And that fantasy had been so much for any partner to live up to that it had driven them all away. I wanted to feel utterly authentic with my lover. Yet I heard Alain de Botton speak disparagingly about why any of us would seek to inflict our whole true self on another poor soul. Nobody wants that I guess. I was coming round to his point of view.

Once, I spoke onstage about the confusing myriad uses of the word love. 'I love my girlfriend and I love chocolate,' I posed. 'One of those is an insatiable, obsessive craving... and the other is how I feel about my girlfriend.' It was a silly, formulaic joke and has probably been said a million times by other comics. Yet there was an insight behind the throwaway daftness. Maybe that lower-key humdrum state was how I was *supposed* to feel about my long-term partner if I really was going to throw myself into the big forever. Maybe she wasn't chocolate but... a salad. Secretly, I still hoped for both. Was a chocolate salad even on life's menu?

For me, the direct inverse of *true* monogamy would probably be serial monogamy, particularly when practised in the non-ethical way demonstrated by Anna. So, I find it troubling that these two opposing concepts have become conflated in our discourse. Opposing forces need to be seen as just that or else Newton's Laws of Motion fly right out the window, along with us and the furniture.

During a slightly testy discussion, I asked a fiercely pro-monogamy pal Julie, 'What would you do if you and your husband stopped having sex?'

Without a breath, she responded, 'Well, I'd dump him and get somebody else!'

I couldn't understand how it was possible to view human beings like this, as replaceable clones. How can one unique individual with all their quirks, flaws and beauty, ever replace another just like that?

But then, we are a society based on commodity. Our thirst for novelty has never been more capacious, fuelled by a tech revolution where new gadgets replace old every year. We need the new thing now. And what's more, we can get it now. This impatience spills over into our romantic lives via dating apps and social media.

It's this harshness that I struggle with, the idea that we discard people like empty crisp packets once we've taken what we need from them. Shouldn't we think about how to fill them back up again and replenish the energy we've drained? Compassion and serial monogamy seem uneasy bedfellows.

I should add that Julie and her husband seem very happily still together. But I know I wouldn't like to be living with that kind of threat hanging over my head.

I wonder if there are two different types of people – those who are adapted to serial monogamy, and seem able to move between partners with barely any gap or emotional fallout, and those who aren't. Clearly, I fall in the latter camp. But where might this duality stem from? Is it possible, in a sense, to be *too* monogamous and end up alone if a partner dies or leaves?

I asked my friend Dr Qazi Rahman, senior lecturer at the Institute of Psychiatry, King's College, London. He said, 'Some people are what we call relationship-oriented as opposed to "single at heart", for example. Those people who have that mating or relationship strategy move on quickly. Whether it's psychologically healthy or not is an open question. But at the other extreme, yes, you can be, as you put it, too monogamous or mono-monogamous – only interested in one partner, the love of your life, and that's it.'

I thought to myself, 'Who is the most mono-monogamous person I know?' It was easy-peasy. My dad. He hasn't seemed to entertain the possibility of a new relationship in the eighteen years and counting since Mum died. Now *that's* fidelity. He occasionally speaks with a slight curious puzzlement about other widowers in the neighbourhood finding new wives.

Yet creaky knee and hip aside, I think he's mostly happy. He has helpful neighbours and more real friends than I probably do in my vast sea of five thousand Facebook acquaintances – all this in spite of, or perhaps because of, his favourite hobbies being the two 'W's of doom, Wagner and walking. He had a lovely marriage for three decades with a bright, funny woman. Why mess up a one-hundred percent track record by rolling the dice again?

Maybe there's a 'super-monogamous' gene that I've inherited. Or at least a learned behaviour or preference for lifelong fidelity with just one mate. Although I've spent much of my life trying to be as different as possible from my father in terms of my career, hobbies and lifestyle, this is undeniably an area of common ground. I respect his loyalty. But we don't discuss it much. Only once we had a frank phone chat about the complexities of love after I was audibly upset about Sarah leaving. 'Relationships are very hard,' he admitted, before telling me a story about Mum once giving his treasured bike away without asking. I had no idea he ever even rode a bike.

Romantics like Dad and me don't sit comfortably at either end of Qazi's relationship-oriented/'single at heart' spectrum. We *are* both people who enjoy time alone. Dad was never happier than when striding off up a mountain. But I think he was mostly happy because Mum and I were waiting for him on a grassy plateau halfway down, where he had left us reading our books and eating cheese and pickle sandwiches, grapefruits and oranges.

In just the same way, I was at my most alive setting off all those times to comedy gigs when I was in a relationship with Sarah. I could do my thing and then catch a late-night train back to her. Gazing out of windows, listening to music, being in love transformed my solitude. The passage of years was marked only by the diminishing size of the device playing those yearning, romantic songs. Being alone becomes beautiful when you've got somewhere and someone to return to. Yet when that person is taken away and the solitude is inescapable, it's a different thing altogether.

Back when I was writing music, pre-Sarah, the prescient closing stanza of a song once read:

'Sometimes it is the sunny days and little victories that hurt the most,

Because they only emphasize you share the best bits of your life with ghosts.'

As an evolutionary strategy, mono-monogamy is admirable but very risky indeed.

Perhaps, then, there are some benefits to serial monogamy after all.

As soon as Susan's initial despair at Anna's departure had dissipated, her Twitter feed became a frenzy of exciting new friends, hobbies and sporting activities. Water-skiing, windsurfing, snowboarding... you name it, she was having a go at it. She even started a 'breakup list', taking on a brand new challenge daily. Her blog rapidly attracted thousands of followers. This was an awakening of epic proportions, a rebirth, albeit one triggered by sadness. I called it 'breakup energy'.

It was as if the loss had catalysed some kind of state of being utterly alive, full of feelings that had, in the words of another of my old songs, *'returned to melt your icy veins, rushing through your cold body, a welcome source of pain.'*

Is there, then, something deadening about being in a long-term relationship, something that removes and distances us from this world, as if trapped behind glass, unable to reach out and touch, taste and experience it?

Is there a way of incorporating this cycle of renewal into our lives, this sense of feeling present and engaged, without the trauma of a separation? Could we have relationship 'gap years' where we go off separately and re-energise ourselves then come back together with the benefits of everything new we've learned?

One of the most famous books on human sexuality and fidelity is *Sex at Dawn*. Right at the start, authors Ryan and Jetha poetically describe serial monogamy as 'stretching before and behind us like an archipelago of failure: isolated islands of transitory happiness in a cold, dark sea of disappointment.' The implication is that land represents the safety of finding a mate.

This binary sense of coupledom as a superior state was

further illustrated in the film *The Lobster* – a satire that unfurled like pure documentary. The people who played by the rules and paired off stayed in a luxury hotel. While the rebels and renegades who opted for single life lived rough in the woods, facing the lashing wind, rain and storms. Yet genuine love seemed ultimately more likely to blossom here than in a high-pressure production line of forced matches.

I wonder, then, if our islands of happiness are actually our times spent single, where we are free to be at our most authentic and electrified. Maybe it is during our relationships that we are submerged and drowning in compromise, silenced by the crashing waves.

CHAPTER 4
THE SILENT HOLIDAY

The bus strained its final gasp up the narrow zigzagging mountain road from Sorrento through lemon trees and olive groves and we stopped at a tiny, remote resort. 'I think this is it,' said Jen hesitantly. A neglected, broken tennis court with no net made me feel foolish for ostentatiously brandishing our rackets. I tried to tuck them discreetly inside my bag. This place was deserted. There wasn't even a hint of a mobile phone signal. 'You could get away with a murder here,' I thought, darkly.

We stood uncertainly outside a sweet little apartment, observing a rusty barbecue, some outdoor seating and a hammock tied between the trees. During peak season, this garden might be buzzing with chatty tourists – couples, families, kids. Yet this near silence, aside from the sound of insects stretching their sleepy wings in the shimmering heat, was perfect. I had completely lost my voice, overdoing it at gigs on top of a throat infection. On the plane, I'd barely been able to croak my food and drink preferences and had been forced to communicate my needs via handwritten notes to Jen. I would have to keep those needs pretty simple for the next few days. She was rather enjoying the chance to prattle on about her work and family uninterrupted.

A wiry, bronzed woman ran over towards us brandishing a comically large key. 'Hello... I'm sorry...'

'Hello. Yes, we're here...' called Jen. I smiled, deferring to her.

'You are sisters?' the woman asked, as she peeked in to check the state of the simple, clean studio before opening the door wider to allow us inside. Jen shrugged amiably and half-acknowledged her incorrect assumption. When foreign hoteliers had come to this conclusion about my relationships with past lovers, it had irked me. It always seemed to reinforce my invisibility as a gay woman. Yet with Jen, this really *was* the most accurate description of our connection. We wouldn't be pushing the two single beds together.

We'd been a team of some kind for two years now. I was starting to feel safer; confident she wasn't going to try and touch me. She knew she had my deep friendship without that needing to be a part of the deal. The annoying thing was that I was just starting to feel alive again sexually. The occasional erotic dream or fantasy seemed less traumatic now as, thankfully, they no longer involved Sarah. Maybe I could revisit sex again? Could I? But I was the one who'd made it explicitly a no-go and Jen had acquiesced. It would be hard to explain a *volte-face* now so I had better stick to my celibate and resolutely non-banging guns.

Nestling at the bottom of my rucksack was a hefty copy of Tristan Taormino's *Opening Up* – the warmest, most accessible introduction to non-conventional relationship structures that a monogamous goody-goody like me could have hoped for. I'd been delighted to find it on the system at Southwark Libraries. It had come up in a search alongside *Opening Up the Bible*. I wryly imagined the author of the latter being quite appalled to be linked in any way to something so radical and sexy.

After a walk along the treacherous road past several boarded-up restaurants to the supermarket, Jen and I cooked delicious pasta – the real Italian stuff, simple, with fresh tomatoes, olive oil and parmesan. Then I sat outside reading as she photographed the green lizards that darted along the hot, stony ground.

'Shall we go to Pompeii one day when you're feeling better?' she asked, squinting in the lowering sun. I nodded.

A friendly, stray, ginger cat sauntered by on the lookout for scraps. We christened him Pussini. Because that's Italian for 'puss', right?

My mute state meant that I couldn't turn to Jen and say, 'oh God, listen to this!' as I learned about the 1960's 'free love' origins of 'polyamory' – a totally new word and world to me – or even as I read about people exactly like us who had a platonic primary partner. Never mind what the *Daily Mail* said, what we were doing was actually a valid relationship form. The only difference in the cases I was reading about was that, unless the two parties were asexual, they tended to have secondary lovers whom they were physically intimate with. Could that be a solution for us? I didn't have enough of a voice to debate it so would have to hold onto that thought for now.

I was chronically behind schedule with writing a show due for an August run in front of critics and industry. I should have been previewing a rough version already. Yet, tucked inside *Opening Up* was my secret weapon: a printout of the early results of an anonymous online survey I'd devised, asking some pretty direct questions about fidelity and what it meant.

Out of a hundred respondents, sixty-two were in a monogamous partnership, twenty-seven were single and defined as monogamous, and the remainder were in more open, or multiple, relationships.

It appeared that the proportion of my mostly-monogamous respondents who admitted to affairs tallied with other surveys referenced by Taormino. It really was close to fifty percent. Shit, that was more than I was expecting. As I always say to couple-heavy audiences, 'If *you're* not cheating, look closely at your partner. Simple maths says it's got to be them.'

Of my first thirty-five participants, sixteen admitted to affairs. That was forty-six percent. The proportion hovered just under half right up until a last-minute flurry of lesbian responses brought it abruptly down to forty percent. They reported the least affairs but a higher turnover of serious partners, one in her fifties having had a dozen exclusive relationships of durations between one and six years. In other words, gay women were incorporating their variety via a fairly extreme form of serial monogamy. Still, we'll talk more about *that* a bit later...

The ratio of people who had actively discussed monogamy with their partner also stayed consistent at around fifty percent. One straight woman wrote, 'Good lord no! It's one thing to do the deed but we're too uptight to actually talk about it. Thank goodness.' A heterosexual man in the eighteen to twenty-four age group was especially candid: 'Yes, we've discussed it, though we've both had affairs and one-night stands secretly, thus breaking the agreed boundaries.' He went on to describe the desire to be more sexually active as 'one of the biggest issues in our relationship'. Also, he admitted he'd be far more forgiving if his girlfriend only engaged in extra-curricular sex with other women. Later, I found out that this is known, somewhat hilariously, as a 'one-penis policy'. I amused myself by sketching a road sign with a penis crossed out, thus giving me a handy motif for navigating through the comedy show. I'd already pictured myself at a crossroads, facing up to the hazards of breakups and affairs. Traffic signs became a theme.

But the key question I'd spent time agonising over was what actually *counts* as infidelity? It seems obvious, until you actually think about it. The options I gave were:

Kissing someone else

Fantasising about someone else

Masturbating while thinking about someone else

Having sex with someone else

Falling in love with someone else without any sexual contact

Looking at porn alone

Text or email flirting with someone else

Staying up all night talking to someone else

Never been in a monogamous relationship

None of these, they can do what they want

Then I left a space underneath for 'other' where people could write what they liked.

The results revealed that my early thoughts that any debate around monogamy would be centred on shagging and swinging were a gross oversimplification of an incredibly sophisticated question.

CHAPTER 5
WHAT IS THIS MONOGAMY?
EMOTIONAL VS SEXUAL

In chapter three, we looked at the origins of the word monogamy. The thing is... it's not really about sex, is it? *Monos gamos* is about marriage, a primary practical commitment. In ancient Greece, prostitution was rife. So I find it hard to believe that they were banging on about sexual exclusivity at all. Not for the men at least. Let's face it – the Greeks had plenty of words for different types of love and connection. Wouldn't it have been *monos eros* if it really was all about finding 'the one'? The romanticised version of lifelong fidelity feels a decidedly more modern invention.

Recognising these nuances, evolutionary biologists began to distinguish between *social* and sexual monogamy. Yet this distinction isn't always recognised by scientists in other fields, or verbalised in the wider public conversation.

The category 'social monogamy' came into play in the

1990s with the advent of genetic fingerprinting. Birds, long held up to be perfect exemplars of monogamy, turned out to be grabbing as much hot, feathery action as they could, as soon as they got a little break from the nest. 'Just going off to get some food for us, darling,' they'd squawk. But it turned out that broods of chicks with many different fathers were just as commonplace as litters of kittens with wildly varying DNA. In the case of cats, however, it's always been a bit more obvious as it results in such different fur colours and markings.

One experiment I read about saw researchers give a group of male red-winged blackbirds vasectomies – rather fiddly work I would imagine. Yet, their female mates still produced offspring and all those cuckolded stepdads were none the wiser. The bird pairs worked together as a tight-knit team, pooling resources and bringing up the chicks. Just as many human couples, they gave the appearance of being monogamous, of having a collaborative, and very practical, bond. That's social monogamy. Sounds pretty close to home, doesn't it?

Another term that only dates from the 1990s is 'polyamory', although it sounds more old-school as it uses the Greek for 'many' and Latin for 'love'. Widely credited with launching the word is the fabulously-named neo-pagan community leader Morning Glory Zell-Ravenheart, who used it in the 1990 essay 'A Bouquet Of Lovers'. It was added by the *Oxford English Dictionary* in 2006 and articles

44

dating from that time quote the original definition as 'the fact of having simultaneous close emotional relationships with two or more other individuals, viewed as an alternative to monogamy'.

This is where things get particularly tricky. Surely having multiple close *emotional* relationships is something that we all do and that can quite happily co-exist alongside some form of monogamy? Aren't we all a bit poly even if we're *sexually* mono? Aside from the time I had a paranoid lover who was so anxious about me talking to anyone else that I once found her secretly scouring my phone bills after retrieving them from my recycling, I've generally felt allowed to have friends outside of a relationship.

Certainly, many of the poly people I've met, and bloggers I've read, place a much higher emphasis on the idea of multiple, consensual, *loving* relationships than on sex. The one who insisted that only physically intimate interactions counted was quite brazen about his thwarted desire to shag me, so we'll discount him for now.

Paradoxically, however, dictionary definitions seem to have shifted emphasis and the current ones I've found now focus on 'the practise of engaging in multiple sexual relationships with the consent of all the people involved'. Or sometimes the words 'intimate' or 'serious' are used to describe the type of simultaneous, ethically and honestly-declared connections that are typical. There's a woolly area here which perhaps allows

45

a little freedom for anyone looking beyond a conventional couple format to define polyamory as they wish. How liberating. It's not to be confused with polygamy, which really is an opposite of monogamy as it refers to having more than one spouse.

In 2014, I was invited to speak at an event in Manchester, cheerily titled Love, Sex and Alienation, alongside academic and activist Don Milligan. He read from his essay 'Human Loving' and poetically described how 'expectations and burden cleave to love like limpets to the bottom of a boat' and ultimately risk destroying it. The way to step off the serial monogamy merry-go-round seemed to me to be to spread this burden of need around different friends, partners and family and alleviate all the stress placed on one person.

These needs range from the sexual to the more emotional, from the romantic to the more platonic and practical. And this is where it gets really interesting. Because, even within self-defined 'monogamous' relationships, we all have very different opinions about which of these needs we can legitimately seek to meet away from our partner. In other words, there's no 'one size fits all' monogamy and no real uniform answer to the question I'd posed in my own survey, 'what counts as infidelity?'

Unsurprisingly, 'having sex with someone else' and 'kissing someone else' ranked the most highly, at ninety-four and seventy-six votes respectively. A few people even seemed to think that adding a location, such as 'in a car', made a difference.

Yet more emotional forms of connection were right up there too, particularly among female respondents. The seventy-three people who ticked 'falling in love with someone else with no sexual contact' or the thirty-one who selected 'staying up all night talking to someone else' would have to have a whole different discussion around fidelity from the people who defined it solely around sexual exclusivity. This last one particularly perturbed my comedian friend Chella as I unveiled it at the end of my Edinburgh show. She rushed up to me as the audience were filing out. 'Does it really count as cheating?' she asked. 'It depends what your partner thinks,' I winked. She didn't seem too reassured.

'Text or email flirting with someone else' was a popular option too, weighing in with a score of sixty-two. One person even added 'watching *Mad Men* with someone else'.

I felt particularly sorry for the partners of the fourteen people who ticked 'masturbating whilst thinking about someone else' and the seven people who nominated 'fantasising about someone else' as an infidelity. If, in the future, we develop ways to read one another's minds, then we are all in a heap of trouble.

The full breakdown of votes, in order of popularity was:

Having sex with someone else – 94

Kissing someone else – 76

Falling in love with someone else without any sexual contact – 73

Text or email flirting with someone else – 62

Staying up all night talking to someone else – 31

Masturbating while thinking about someone else – 14

Fantasising about someone else – 7

Looking at porn alone – 4

None of these, they can do what they want – 3

Never been in a monogamous relationship – 2

Admittedly, this was a small sample of a hundred people. I tweeted the link to a variety of groups to aim for a spread of respondents across genders, ages and sexualities, yet I can't guarantee complete randomness. I'm a humble comedian with no serious funding to allow me to make this research my full-time job. Still, the complex patterns that start to emerge are hard to ignore. My friend Liz Bentley has worked for many years as a therapist by day and a brilliantly dark poet and comedian by night. In an email chat about the survey, she commented, 'Our society likes everything to be black and white but it isn't that simple. We are all individual human beings. Expectations are sold to us by systems that are impossible to fit into on a constant basis.'

Discussing the results with me, Qazi Rahman said, 'This is perfectly consistent with the biology and psychology of relationships which says that people worry more about their partners committing sexual or emotional infidelity than anything else. Most people endorsed the top three or four responses in your survey and then the percentages dropped off significantly – which means that staying up all night talking to someone, masturbating, watching porn and fantasising are not important definitions of cheating.'

He continued, 'Men tend to worry more about sexual infidelity and women emotional. So I wonder if you had more men in your survey which is why "having sex with someone else" got the highest endorsement.'

I went back to check the gender split. The respondents were actually sixty percent female. But the fact that twenty-three of those identified as lesbian, a much higher proportion than you would get in a typical random group of women, may well have skewed the result. We surmised that gay women might have a more 'masculine' outlook on infidelity, taking a dimmer view on sexual straying than on emotional non-exclusivity. Emotional forms of non-monogamy, whether labelled as such or not, tend to be common within the community. Close romantic friendships or ongoing connections with ex-partners are typical. Bonds between gay women are strong. So perhaps this is why these behaviours might be perceived differently by heterosexual women whose male partners were in love with other women.

However, Qazi also went on to tell me that 'when you interview people who actually experienced their partners cheating on them, both sexes say it was the emotional aspect (falling in love with someone else) that was the worst. So this shows a difference between when people think about what they would find worse in a hypothetical situation versus when it actually happens to them.'

Although my 2010 show The Science Of Sex predated my questioning of monogamy, the finale was an impassioned speech, set to Eg White's 'There's Going To Be Someone', urging couples to communicate better. If fidelity really was as confusing as it now seemed to be, that message suddenly felt more important than ever.

CHAPTER 6

POLY STORIES: INFINITE CREDIT

Once I'd started posting about my new show on social media and doing radio interviews, all sorts of non-monogamists started popping out of the woodwork. Some were fellow performers who I'd always assumed to be monogamous. Until recently, having multiple relationships wasn't something you could shout about. Many were hard to pin down for interviews, due to their hectic romantic schedules. One woman emailed me saying, 'I think I've got an evening in June.' This was in early April. But it wasn't too long before I was having a Facebook chat with forty-year-old comedian friend Kate Smurthwaite and her forty-five-year-old partner James Farr and hearing, first from her, how they'd gone about opening up their relationship...

'We met about four years ago in a bar. Initially we were quite determined for the relationship to stay casual. We

talked a lot about not wanting to be monogamous and resisted moving in together for largely that reason. But then James and his son were struggling with the rent in their unsuitable flat. I couldn't leave them like that so they moved in with me. We still talked about being open but in practice there wasn't much else going on.

Then a flirting-after-a-show situation turned a bit more serious and I started spending some time with a guy. I didn't feel that I had to ask permission or anything. Our relationship's never been like that. But I was being honest and saying "I'm going to stay out tonight in town with him." After a while this guy was very into me and was sending me a ton of over-the-top messages. Because James and I work so closely together, he saw them and asked me to tell him what was going on.

So we had a big chat. Mostly I reassured him that I wasn't about to leave. During said chat we rewrote the "rules" to an overt "do ask, do tell" policy – which suits me much, much better. I don't like half-secrets and if another partner is being a dick I want to come home and tell James about it. Since then James has been on OK Cupid and met a second regular partner. And not long after that I met a guy at a sex party, started meeting up with him regularly and it's turned into a secondary relationship.'

Initially, I felt a tiny bit sorry for the first flirting-after-a-show guy. Maybe he really had developed intense feelings and it was fair enough to express them. But then, I haven't seen the messages. Maybe I'm just too much of a starry-eyed idealist who wants everyone's love to be heard and received. Besides, inequality of feeling happens all the time in monogamous relationships and is hardly an exclusively poly problem.

Even though Kate's the one I've enjoyed gigging with for years on the circuit, it was James' version of the story that particularly triggered my empathy and almost made me wish that I was straight and could ask him out on a date. If men had seemed this emotionally open twenty years ago, things might have been different...

'When we first met, we were both keen to keep it light and casual. I was now over forty, had had more than enough of painful breakups and was still a little raw from the most recent one. I was determined to be steely-hearted and never allow myself to get in a position to be hurt again. So the notion of it being open was there.

Then it became apparent that the relationship was getting more meaningful. So much for never allowing my heart to melt again! However, at no time did I feel that inferred a shift towards monogamy. I simply wasn't really looking for anyone else, and if Kate was seeing other people I didn't know I kind of assumed it was likely to happen. She travels up and down the country, performing to adoring fans, staying overnight in hotels regularly. I would be naive to assume it wasn't a possibility.

However, when I stumbled on those messages from that

guy, it was at a time when I was feeling pretty down. The "don't ask don't tell" approach, which we'd probably only adopted as something of a convenient default, suddenly felt threatening. Who was he? What were his motives? Why were they being so intimate? What did he have that I didn't? So that forced us to have a long talk, mostly to allay fears. But it seemed like a good time to lay down proper ground rules and agree that the "do ask, do tell" approach was a better way forward. I am much more comfortable with us having all our cards on the table. It feels less duplicitous. Kate and I have got to where we are not quite by design, but often through being clumsy or occasionally unintentionally hurtful. But always at the heart of the relationship there is love and the desire to be honest, respectful and understanding.'

He went on to tell me the significance of Tom Stoppard's The Real Thing, after he performed in an Am-dram production of it soon after Kate and he started dating. His character Henry was a playwright struggling to comprehend love and the fact that his partner was probably having an affair.

'There's one particular line that I think best defines our relationship that we both keep coming back to: "Be indulgent, negligent, preoccupied, premenstrual... Your credit is infinite, I'm yours, I'm committed..."

I love the concept of infinite credit in a relationship. We will both occasionally fuck up, but we both understand and accept that.'

Putting aside for a moment the possibilities for abuse of this idea if it fell into the wrong hands and the credit didn't work both ways, I rather like it too. By contrast, monogamy seems a bit miserly. I've spent years policing and limiting partners' behaviours, resulting in ridiculous back-and-forth tit-for-tat exchanges of faux-threats like, 'If you so much as look at someone else, I'll gouge your eyes out with a spoon.' Or 'If I catch you whispering sweet nothings to someone, I'll create a SoundCloud page just of you snoring.' Although these bombs were dropped during intentionally silly verbal jousting matches, they reinforced a stifling sensibility that even a bit of harmless flirting was not to be tolerated. And, well, if you have to shut down your sexual self to that extent, how the hell can you muster up any flirtatious energy for your partner?

The trouble with defining extra-partner sex as an automatic 'end-of-all-worlds', even before it happens, is that you've then got no room for manoeuvre when it does. You have to smash things, change the locks and throw all their clothes into the garden. Because that's what you've said you would do. You're setting yourself up for a life of paranoia and potential isolation, all other humans viewed through the grimy lens of sexual competition and kept at a distance. Kate and James seemed to have freed themselves from all of this bullshit anxiety and jealousy quite spectacularly. He continued:

There will always be someone better looking, funnier,

richer and sexier and so on but they'll never be "us". Rather than go through our time together worrying about if and when the other will run off with one of these arbitrary ideals, we get on with the business of being soulmates and embrace the other's happiness wherever they find it.'

Enjoying the happiness a lover finds with other partners is sometimes known as 'compersion' or, particularly in the UK, 'frubbly'. This latter term sounds a bit like a children's ice lolly to me, but I love the idea.

Even in ethical non-monogamy it's still very common, almost more so given the level of mature discussion it prompts, to define some kind of relationship 'rules'. I asked Kate what theirs were:

'The main "rule" is if James has women over and they sleep in our bed, he changes the sheets afterwards. I never have men/partners home – or at least it's not something I've ever done so far. I spend half my life in hotel rooms. Or I can afford a hotel if I want to stay out with someone. If I'm going to be away, sometimes James has his other partner over and then I come home to nice clean sheets. Once I stayed on a friend's sofa after my plans fell through so that James wouldn't have to cancel his date.'

Then James added:

'It was initially a misgiving of mine that Kate seemed to have a world of opportunities for things to happen and the means to accommodate them when they did. This imbalance seemed unfair. But all I had to do was ask about the

possibility of bringing someone back to our house, our bed, and she was totally understanding and totally cool about it. She rocks!'

But, I asked Kate, are the other connections only about sex or something more?

'I would say I'm mostly looking for sex but when that goes well there's definitely room for something else to form, something emotional. It'd be odd to see someone regularly without connecting with them. Scott, my secondary partner, and I go for meals, boat trips and days out. If I'm gigging out of town and the promoter has paid for a nice hotel, I hate to waste it so, if James is busy or doesn't fancy it, I'll take Scott if I can.'

This hit home as I recalled all the 'plus one' VIP festival tickets that had gone begging when I'd had gigs and nobody to take. Jen has only ever come fairly begrudgingly as she hates muddy, outdoors-y stuff and has usually insisted on leaving before the band I want to see. To be honest, finding someone to go to festivals with is more important to me than finding someone to have sex with. But if I have to have sex in order to get a proper, dedicated festival buddy, I guess I'll consider it.

Opening up was starting to sound like a pretty awesome idea. I asked Kate what effect it had had on their central partnership:

'It's even better. It means I'm not driven mad if James isn't in the mood for sex. And it means I know he's getting some even if I'm tired or out of town.'

I was at a party recently with a fellow comedian who saw Kate and James together more frequently than I did. She remarked that she'd never seen them looking so loved up and tactile. So something is clearly working better than monogamy ever did for them. Kate describes herself as 'naturally poly' and talks of dumping 'some perfectly lovely men' in her twenties when she thought that being frequently unfaithful was a sign something wasn't right.

Conversely James has never been unfaithful:

'I think I was pretty vanilla before. I've had many frustrating situations in relationships where I've been the one constantly looking for sex and my partner not being into it. I never felt the urge to cheat on them but I wish I'd been braver and more aware of polyamory sooner. It might even have saved a couple of relationships. But then... I wouldn't be here now with Kate, or for that matter with my secondary partner G. So although I'm late to the party I'm very happy with my lot.'

In all the heterosexual open relationships I discovered, I was intrigued to find that the rejection of monogamy was often primarily driven by the woman. After my show in Edinburgh, I even chatted to two women whose husbands quite happily allowed them to sleep with other lovers but didn't want to pursue these freedoms themselves.

One of them, Samantha, discussed it less than a year into her marriage and started to see a regular on-off boyfriend. She said:

'I'd like to meet someone I can connect with on all levels: emotionally, sexually, intellectually and spiritually. That's a big ask, which is why I don't know if monogamy is realistic: whether one person can meet all my needs and vice versa. I think I could be monogamous if I could connect that intimately with one person and we had a stable foundation. By that I mean financial stability, a secure home and a strong support network outside of the relationship.'

When I expressed my own surprise that it seemed to be women who were often driving, and thriving in non-monogamy, she nodded and said,

'Yeah, I always thought it was men who were more likely to seek sex out but wonder now if that is just a popular media and cultural myth.'

In fact, a 2011 Dutch survey of business executives found that income, status and position on the corporate ladder were far greater indicators of a drive to seek out additional sexual partners than gender.

CHAPTER 7

THE TEARS OF A CLOWN

'I just get sad sometimes because of life, because of bad things happening, like Mum dying or breakups or whatever...'

I was having a coffee with Lynne Parker, founder of the Funny Women Awards and one of the key comedy-industry people responsible for inspiring me to take this career path. She looked straight at me, caringly, wanting me to work it out.

'But maybe those things are triggers, Rosie, for something underlying'.

Oh.

I went to a party where friends asked if I was OK, because my recent Facebook posts had all seemed really vulnerable. That day, I'd had a good day, a creative day full of ideas and plans. 'I feel great,' I said, beaming, holding court with a funny story. One of the party hosts, Noelle, put her arm around me tenderly and said, completely out of the blue, 'Are you bipolar, Rosie?'

Oh.

I read *Attitude* editor Matthew Todd's incredible and urgent book *Straight Jacket: How to be Gay and Happy*. In a chapter entitled 'Coming Out of Denial', he lists questions about food, alcohol and drugs that various Twelve Steps fellowships ask in order to determine where potential problems lie. He says, 'If you've answered yes to three or more of these questions, then there is a very strong chance you have a problem that you might wish to do something about.' My eyes fell on the eight questions under the heading 'Problem with love addiction?' I instinctively answered 'yes' to all eight.

Oh.

While I was pretty sure that many of the people I'd met on my poly journey were in perfectly fine mental health and were making a very positive choice that genuinely worked for them, I had to acknowledge that my own questioning of monogamy had been catalysed by an immense sense of being let down. I wasn't in a good place emotionally. My profound feeling of being alone in the world was exacerbated and amplified by the weary cycle of serial monogamy. Every few years, a person would come along and make huge proclamations about solving everything and then, after about six weeks, reveal that they can't do any such thing.

I'd always thought of myself as pretty robust. I accepted my ups and downs. That was the energy that fired my creativity. That was all part of the deal with being a performer, wasn't it? I once heard Ruby Wax speaking about lows so debilitating she could barely get out of bed for days. I wasn't really like that. I could pretty much always get out of bed and take life on. Getting out of a relationship was my problem. I was trapped, held to ransom by my own loneliness and fear of the same old pattern repeating.

My response was always to fight for a solution. That was how I had learned to function with whatever form of low-level depression I was dealing with.

In fact, Sarah had cited my resilience as one of the reasons she couldn't bear to be with me. I made *her* feel inadequate. Yet my strength had come from her, from my passionate desire for her. Stripped of that purpose, I was like Samson without hair. My secret weapon had gone. Now I was the one in tears in the supermarket for no apparent reason.

This time, I had fallen so far into my pool of grief that ice had formed above my head. I couldn't resurface and reinvent myself, normally the part I excelled at. Yet New Year's Eve 2013 represented a line in the sand, an absolute. Three years of feeling inauthentic and miserable was enough. The promise and potential of 2014 glistened like a shining prize, hovering just above the melting, thinning ice. Something was shifting. It was a slow thaw. But it was real.

Jen and I strolled to the top of Hampstead Heath, laden with flasks of mulled wine, to watch fireworks cascade across the city we both loved. A few other disparate groups of people played tinny music on competing portable stereos, providing an odd discordant soundtrack quite different to the official one playing out on the banks of the Thames. We stared out into the blackness for a few moments as the ghostly vapour trails faded, as if they might signal a way forward for us.

I was enjoying spending time in north London. 'Living apart together' was working for us. Weekends were mostly spent at Jen's Kentish Town flat, nicknamed 'the cloud' due to its pristine whiteness. I did my fair share of domestic chores and had a sense of it being our shared space. The moment she had pressed a set of keys into my hand on a Northern Line Tube carriage was the sole occasion she had made my tummy flip. She represented safety, something I desperately needed... yet felt suffocated by. We spent less time at my eccentric, scuzzy and cold Peckham studio, nicknamed 'the den'. If Jen did make it there, it was usually to help me clear some of my clutter. My old life was systematically being thrown out, physically and spiritually.

It was a horrendous cliché to have a 'big relationship talk' at New Year. I didn't want to break up with Jen. I'd tried that before and she hadn't agreed. After what Sarah had inflicted on me, I just couldn't do that to someone against their will. It was too brutal, too barbaric, too violent. There had been no kindness in Sarah's cruelty. Besides, I really *wanted* to have a relationship with Jen. Just not the one we had found ourselves having. We were fixed in an unhelpful dynamic, defined by my state of unhappiness. Could we start again?

Every time I proposed a reinvention of 'us', Jen had blocked it by saying 'we are where we are.' It was her way of denying me a chance at turning the clock back. It seemed unfair. But I wanted to try again to be heard.

Back in her cosy lounge, I broke the silence.

'I got into this relationship too quickly. I do want to be with you. But I needed to find myself again, find my feet, my sexuality. Now I don't know how. I need to explore it.'

Jen sighed, 'We've been through this before. It's not like I forced you to go out with me.'

'I know. I felt rushed. Not by you. But just by... life.'

It was true. I had been in such a state of disempowerment when we met that I was simply not in a position to make a decision about something as important as a potential life partner. Relationships are always a gamble. Yet I was a gambler with no chips left. I had nothing except my sexual currency left to bargain with. It was my only credit.

'Why don't we have a month of space? We can both do what we want. Then we get back together,' Jen said.

This sounded perfect. I'd negotiated a chance to breathe and think. But, by making the suggestion for a gap month she was able to feel some control over it.

65

Our January space was punctured by the announcement of an Oxford University study into the psychology of comedians. The headline finding was that we had 'high levels of psychotic traits' and an unusual combination of introversion and extraversion. Apparently we differed from actors particularly in this high introversion factor. This was what interested me, as the aspect they were particularly investigating was 'a reduced ability to feel social and physical pleasure, including an avoidance of intimacy.' I was certainly struggling to find intimacy, although I craved and chased it as opposed to avoiding it.

Jen posted a link to the survey results on my Facebook wall with the message 'This explains a lot! xx.' It felt like she was coming to terms with the fact that she wasn't with someone straightforward. Loving a creative had its complexities. If she understood this, it made me feel better. It prompted a rekindling. We sent one another endless texts and pictures of Moomins, after bonding over watching a Tove Jansson documentary together.

My show Nineties Woman received Arts Council funding, something I'd been trying for and failing at for two years. I could now afford to work with a director, Colin. Feeling less alone in my creative world made me feel more connected in the rest of my life.

'Well done, doll,' said Jen. 'Things are looking up.'

I sold all my old guitars, amps and CDs, relics of my old life as a musician. And when my landlord tried to hike up the rent for my dilapidated flat, we decided to move in together. We found a lovely house on three levels for a relatively good rent close to Brockwell Park and around the corner from one of my oldest friends. We chose furniture together and bounced on beds in bed shops, dreaming of fantasy future pets including a dachshund called Geraldine.

It was hardly the stuff of textbook romance. But it felt right. Ambiguous as our relationship was, I wanted to live with her and hoped it would make everything right. Even the intimacy.

CHAPTER 8

MORE POLY STORIES:

RUNNING THROUGH THE HOUSE OPENING UP THE BLINDS

Thirty-three-year-old writer and performer friend Dave Pickering opened up his relationship with his girlfriend after they'd been together for eleven years. They met on their first day at uni, both having had one significant teenage relationship.

I chatted with him at Brixton Ritzy ahead of a storytelling night he was hosting. He told me that the decision to make this big change came from a sense of not wanting to break up, coupled with knowing that lies and affairs would be something they couldn't forgive.

'Sex was a complicated thing for us for years. I wasn't capable of dealing with that in an emotionally mature way. I felt ugly and rejected. Then I got into Dan Savage's podcast and queer, kink and open relationships all flooded into my consciousness.'

He described an absolute transformation that took place, in terms of their intimacy, his personal self-confidence and how he began to think about sex. For a man who'd always considered himself 'straight-ish', this was revolutionary.

'It was like running through the house opening up the blinds. It made me a better performer, able to reach into more personal stuff. It's also opened up how I think about sex. Penis in vagina isn't the only kind. I've questioned so many things about gender, sex, the trans experience...'

Although his partner was the one to suggest the new arrangement – something that he thought helped them when they came out to family and friends – he was the first to act on it. The process began with a slight bump, however, when he did so before they'd both 'officially' agreed:

'She was initially shocked and betrayed but then relieved that she didn't have to be the one who started it. Dealing with it live prepares you for the eventuality. Clearing it in advance isn't always workable.'

He described that first encounter as a huge relief and release. Yet he was simultaneously struck by the sheer 'normality of it'. The number of people he'd slept grew to ten, a number which he never thought would be likely.

They have always answered any questions the other asks about experiences with other lovers:

'How much she wants to know about sex or romance is up to her. I'm more interested in details. She's not. Part of it turns me on, yet I do feel jealousy. I remember I got a text

the first time saying, "It's happened!" I was making Lego with my niece and I remember thinking it was good to be distracted.'

After three years of openness, he felt that sex with his girlfriend had become closer and 'un-weaponised':

'She can talk about what she wants to do rather than what she might feel obligated to. There are things on the sexual platter now that weren't before. We've got stronger together and made more time for each other.

We're best friends and describe each other as partners and other connections as lovers. Even if we see someone regularly, we're not interested in other life partners. We're also "fluid-bonded", in that we don't use protection with one another but do with other people.

If either of us ever does want to return to monogamy, we can.'

***

So far, I'd heard from couples who had experienced barely any hurdles with negotiating openness – as both of them had wanted it. But what happens when one half of a partnership is strictly monogamous and the other isn't, effectively making them a 'mono-poly' couple? I was fascinated when forty-eight-year-old Catherine contacted me to tell me that was the setup in her two-year relationship with fifty-three-year-old Emma.

Emerging from a couple of decades on the serial monogamy treadmill and a particularly painful breakup,

71

Catherine had pretty much sworn off romantic relationships. 'I'd had three that lasted four or five years. And for the first time in my life I was thinking, "I really don't want that." But there's nothing more likely to fuck up your plans... than making plans.'

Her intentions went awry when she met Emma, after being put in touch by a mutual friend, and felt 'a deep recognition, a complete sense of ... "oh, of course... it's you"... and that was it. We effectively "married" on sight.'

So far, so fairytale... until an intriguing and challenging question emerged for them both. Were they in a monogamous relationship? For Catherine, 'sexual exclusivity had always been a requirement.' Then, one month into the partnership, they spent a summer together in Greece. 'Emma started talking about the difficulties of being in a monogamous relationship. It was really pissing me off and I was thinking, "Can you stop mentioning non-monogamy every other word, please?" It wasn't that she wanted to have sex with other people. The issue was that she *didn't* want to and she felt really freaked out by that.'

While they clearly had 'that real animal attraction... it's so otherly, like a strong, deep, chemical reaction', it became clear that they each had different ways of expressing and understanding their sexuality. 'Mine is more internalised whereas hers is an outwards, sensual interaction with the world.'

Catherine's deepest fears and jealousies were stirred up

when Emma invited a free-spirited, lithe intellectual to stay for a week. This woman was cycling across Europe alone and had been put in contact by mutual friends. Although Catherine was certain that Emma 'would never have a sexually intimate encounter with another person without my consent beforehand', it was clear that she had an emotional closeness with the new house guest.

Catherine started to reconsider more broadly what fidelity was. 'Why would you worry about sexual exclusivity when they might have a really deep conversation that they don't tell you about? I was *so* jealous. I had a really primal "who's eating my porridge?" response to it.'

This experience forced her to re-evaluate her position on something she'd always felt was pretty fixed. 'Ultimately, it didn't make me feel any less loved. There was actually *more* love available because she was more alive, challenged and engaged. So I've been through this radical change. I could now entertain the idea of Emma having a fling with someone else. Psychologically, she needs to leave that possibility there. It's great that we are liberated enough to have these conversations.'

Catherine's new stance had come about largely as a result of hating the idea of restricting the woman she loves. 'Do I really want to be the reason that she missed out on a moment of tenderness? But... do I have the emotional resources to cope with that reality?'

I asked how she felt about the possibility of that future

reality. 'I dread it,' she said, unequivocally. 'I would have to put my money where my mouth is. I'd say "yes" but I don't know if I could pay the price. I would ask for a marriage, I think, so that we have a solid commitment and rules around our core relationship. But I can see now how it could potentially add something to our lives. I appreciate who she is beyond my need of her.'

***

In some parts of the world where conventional views of relationships hold even firmer than they do in the UK, I can see how alternatives might be particularly desirable. My twenty-seven-year-old bisexual Facebook friend Stephanie, who lives in Singapore, got in touch with a picture of being poly there:

It's still a relatively new, foreign concept here. In my experience, it's inextricably linked to class. It's mainly people who have a certain level of education and privilege who are aware of the theory and lifestyle.

One reason why I want to be poly is because I find relationship culture in Singapore to be toxic, among both straight and queer communities. There is a huge amount of possessiveness and jealousy. People still hold very traditional views towards the need for being in serious monogamous relationships and eventually marriage.

Most people live with their parents until then. If you are under thirty-five, you can only register to buy a cheaper government flat if you are about to get married. I'm not saying that everyone gets married in order to move out of the parents' home – but it's a pretty big motivation. People also work really hard, averaging nine to twelve hour days. Some friends say, "you might as well get married, at least to have someone to come home to in the few hours between work days." It's an insanely depressing lifestyle to think about, but which I understand is the reality for many people here.

This is not to say polyamory doesn't exist in Singapore. Some people within the kink community have formed a poly meet-up group. The first and only meeting I went to was awkward because it was organised by my ex and her then-partner. I attended with my then-partner. The four of us were the only queer couples in the group.

The workshop was facilitated by a straight, white man who was very well-known within the kink community. Most of the other people were expats, European or American. We found the discussion useful but very straight-centric and did not take into consideration any of the issues we faced as young people from Singapore who still lived with our parents and did not have expat jobs.

I did keep in touch with one guy from the group, who seemed the most sex-positive and had politics that matched ours. He is very openly poly at his school and says his classmates are often shocked when he tells them about it. His partner says her friends keep telling her that she is being mistreated.'

Sex-positivity is, broadly speaking, an ideology that all sex, as long as it is healthy and consensual, is a fundamentally good thing. It seemed to apply across all of the poly and kink groups I found. However, as Stephanie articulates above, I was starting to find that, while open-minded, it was a largely hetero-dominated world.

Back here in London, younger lesbian couples I've spoken to seem theoretically to agree openness but find limited opportunity to act upon it in practice. Thirty-year-old writer, activist and artist Sam Dodd has become a friend on the feminist cabaret circuit and on social media. We bonded over a shared queasiness around same-sex marriage and an enveloping sense of normativity encroaching on the queer community.

Her and partner Bethan discussed ethical non-monogamy two years ago, at the start of their relationship. She told me, 'We talked about it partly because we were both freaked out by how much we liked each other and we didn't want to fuck it up.' It wasn't that they were actively looking but acknowledged that the time may come. They set some ground rules ready for when or if the situation arose: 'Nobody that the other one knows and no more than three times with the same person. But... as a lesbian, it's much more difficult to find a free and easy partner.'

That's exactly what I'd been thinking...

CHAPTER 9

HOT STUFF: LET'S DO SOMETHING

Sex seemed the only thing that was really broken in my relationship with Jen. I couldn't understand why so many good connections lived or died by it. We spent weekends strolling across Brockwell Park to browse the Herne Hill markets, maybe taking in a film at the Ritzy. We were companions. To some extent, I was happy.

Yet I couldn't help but think that if only I could rediscover my sexuality and then find a way to connect to Jen on that level, we could have it all. We could be like all those other couples, relentlessly showing off how *in* love they were.

I'd been too much of a monogamous prude to realise, but lesbians are sometimes allowed to have casual sex – once every two months apparently. That's how frequently The Locker Room, a gay sauna just off south London's leafy, affluent Cleaver Square, is hijacked by the women. Now that I was writing a show on sex and fidelity, I could visit under the comforting guise of 'research'. I'd been told tales of wild excess about what went on there, behind the clouds of steam and sweat, by gay male friends. Would women behave with similar animalistic abandon?

I heard about the sporadic women's event through my friend Bel, who described herself as 'solo poly' and explained this as 'engaging in multiple, ethically non-exclusive relationships while abandoning the hierarchical structure of a primary relationship'. Although she cared very much for her lovers and friends, her key commitment was to herself and her own path. To remind herself of this, she wore a single wedding ring around her neck on a chain. She had effectively married herself. To her, a lesbian sauna was no big deal. She had nobody to report her whereabouts to, and the partners she was with would totally get it anyway.

Whereas, to me, its very existence was a big neon sign informing me just what a clueless and closed-minded idiot I was. I didn't dare fantasise about actually doing anything remotely sexual with a complete stranger in a public space. But the mere act of putting myself in this environment was enough to start pushing at the oppressive asexual straightjacket I'd found myself tied up in for the last few years.

Bel and I agreed not to cramp one another's style. I would leave her to her own devices... or vices. Yet if I was in any way uncomfortable, I was to go and discreetly belch in her ear. It was the most ridiculous safe word ever. I wasn't even sure if I could belch on demand. Yet she had once heard of a friend and his wife using it as a code and the idea had tickled her enough to copy it.

An amiable, bespectacled butch, who seemed to be in charge, proposed an icebreaker game in the cramped bar upstairs. Even though most of us were still clothed and sipping milky tea from polystyrene cups there was a giggly frisson, the airless space rich with pheromones.

The butch clapped her hands like a PE mistress rounding up her girls and explained that we must speak to the person next to us. Then when she rang a bell, switch our attention to somebody else. I enquired if the bell system would be employed later on, encouraging us to rotate partner once we had started getting off with each other. This got a big laugh. I could've happily gone home then.

But then a slender, toned woman a few years my senior strutted over. 'I'm Helen,' she purred, fluttering eyelashes thick with mascara, browny-greying curls cascading around long earrings, droplets of silver pointing down to her glistening neck and chest.

'Rosie,' I said, instinctively offering a handshake, a formal and robust greeting to legitimise what might follow.

'What do you want to do tonight?'

Oh God. I hadn't prepared for this question. I thought to myself, I wouldn't mind an intelligent discussion on

79

Britain's role in the European Union. Instead I gulped. I looked over at Bel, and wondered if I could employ our code this early into the evening.

A fear gripped me that I hadn't felt since I was a teenager and Mum's friend Monica had asked me what I wanted to do when I grew up. How can you answer? How does anyone know? This was the same. If I say 'spanking' just for the hell of it, she might say, 'I'm into that. Let's go.' I might have to go through with it just out of politeness.

Fortunately the bell rang. A pretty Asian femme barely half my age whirled round to catch my eye, long painted fingernails giving her sexual tourism away.

'You look like a film star,' she proclaimed.

'Thanks,' I said, 'which one?'

'I don't know,' she laughed.

This was immediately more comfortable to me than the first situation with 'Helen'. This girl clearly had no idea what she was doing, which meant that I wouldn't be exposed as not knowing what I was doing either.

Once we descended to the steamy, dimly-lit basement, a blonde woman started nonchalantly flicking through a magazine. A strange mix of aloof and slutty, she pulled down her bikini top to rest underneath her breasts. Then, in a moment of OCD, she started folding towels and tidying.

This was hardly the hedonistic gang bang I'd anticipated. I imagined reporting back to my friend Don, the one person

I'd told where I was in case I died and somebody had to be contacted.

'What happened?' he'd say, expectantly.

'Nothing,' I'd say.

But then the Asian girl leaned forward from the bench above me and whispered, 'Let's do something.'

Silently, I took her hand and led her out to the shower. After being in the cosy cocoon of the sauna, however, emerging into the draughty corridor felt like stepping into a blizzard naked. How do gay men cope with this temperature change?

We turned on the shower and tried to kiss under its dribbly warmth. But it was on a timer. The water kept stopping.

'Let's go to the steam room,' she suggested, not to be defeated.

The steam room was insanely hot, like climbing inside a kettle. There's no way I would be able to stay in there long enough to make a woman orgasm. That shit takes time.

We started kissing awkwardly, like kids playing spin the bottle.

Then, as the steam parted, I saw a familiar-looking face watching.

I tried to concentrate on kissing but kept looking over.

'Who is she... ?' I asked myself, then remembered. 'Oooh yes. She's a regular at my gigs who often tweets me afterwards with not entirely welcome feedback.'

I imagined her judging me this time, holding up a score card.

'Hi Rosie.'

'Hi,' I blurted, sitting upright.

We all started chatting, as women do. Then went upstairs for another cup of milky tea.

CHAPTER 10
SEX, CONSENT AND PHANTOM DICKS

It was depressingly clear to me that, even if a quick fix of anonymous sex had been less awkwardly available, it was the last thing I was really searching for. If only I was programmed like some of my gay male friends and it really was that simple. If I was seeking Jen's permission, or perhaps wider society's permission, to be non-monogamous, it was emotionally so rather than sexually.

For my sins, I'm a romantic. Sex feels empty and meaningless without connection. It could never, would never compare to music, poetry or walking along the sea's edge at sunset.

Yet most people hold up sex as the gateway to emotional intimacy. Sometimes, I would just love to have the level of intellectual closeness we experience post-orgasm without actually having to go through with the sex. I'm able to reach that intensity anyway. It's part of my job to look inside myself and be vulnerable. But, in my experience thus far, I've struggled to find anyone happy to venture there with me until they've secured exclusive, regular access to my naked body.

I realise now that a fairly hefty portion of the sex I've had in my lifetime I haven't actually actively consented to. I just craved a good conversation. I feel that I've been coerced by a societal structure that doesn't work for me. In near to twenty-five years of monogamous relationships with both women and a few, fleeting men, the actual word consent has never been uttered.

Once I took a woman home after a boozy trip to now-defunct lesbian drinking den The Candy Bar. Back in my bedroom, I was enjoying snogging someone I barely knew, chatting and drinking more wine. But then something changed. She started sifting through my belongings and CDs in a way that felt invasive. She was in my space yet felt the right to rummage through my clothes. She reached out for my guitar.

'Please don't touch that, it's really expensive,' I whispered, so that she could only just hear it.

She settled back onto the bed with me. I looked up and down her solid arms, suddenly aware of how much bigger than me she was. I didn't want to think the thought that entered my head... the idea that one woman might assault another, a fellow sister. That didn't happen, right?

'Can we just go to sleep?' I yawned, feigning sudden exhaustion.

But we didn't go to sleep. We fucked. Because that was just easier and less scary than explaining that I'd gone off the idea. I hated myself a little for being that out of control of my own boundaries.

Because monogamous relationships rest on a sweeping assumption about fidelity, too many assumptions are often made about other really precious things like sexual preference and consent. That's one of the things that appeals to me about being poly. Communication around consent is an inherent part of the process, both in terms of what you do with other people and what you do with each other. Being forced to talk can only be a good thing.

The irony isn't lost on me that my personal retreat from physical intimacy seemed to go hand in hand with inadvertently setting up my professional self as a champion of sexual and romantic freedom, a spokesperson for polyamory. Once word had got around about my show title, requests flooded in from radio producers, TV shows, bloggers and magazines all keen for me to spill the beans on my apparent hedonistic lifestyle. I tried to keep the focus on the theoretical and the emotional, much to the disappointment of some.

On Radio 4's short-lived late-night discussion series *Summer Nights*, I tried to argue with Susie Orbach, Suzi Godson and others about what actually counts as sex. I posited that I'd had conversations with friends about sex that had proved way more intensely arousing than much of the actual, real action I'd had. Couldn't I claim those experiences as sexual if I wanted to? The idea of focusing any definition of sex around genitals, even if we've moved beyond the concept of those genitals needing to comprise one penis and one vagina, seemed exclusive. What about people who sought to find intimacy in other ways? What if they were dysphoric about their bodies because they were trans or had been raped or had an eating disorder? Sadly, I felt too shouted down to express any of this.

I started to feel a troubling disconnect from my own body and to fantasise that I could grow a penis whenever I wanted to. I could almost feel it throbbing in my pants, a phantom limb I was sure must have been there once. I'd read that snails were hermaphrodites and had a choice whenever they had sex whether they were going to act as the male or the female. 'How wonderful to have a choice,' I thought, sick of being trapped and limited by my biology into a role. The clitoris is essentially made of the same tissue, after all. How stupidly unhelpful that it's all locked away inside, waiting to receive stimulation rather than protruding outwards ready to be active.

I recalled Richard Herring once talking onstage about lesbian sex and imagining two women running at each other from opposite corners of the room and crashing vaginas together. He was articulating my problem. I wanted some way that female genitals could morph shape and fuse together temporarily. But I felt I'd tried every uncomfortable scissoring position and just ended up in a tangle of frustration.

When Emily Dubberly appeared on my radio show to speak about her book on sexual fantasies, I asked her afterwards about my sudden and unexpected cock-envy. 'Loads of women get that,' she said, 'it's usually when they want to regain sexual control.' Ah, so I wasn't really confused about my gender identity then... just a bloody control freak.

The irony is that lesbian sex should feel like a level playing field. Both partners have the same biology. The critical problem is that it's impossible to concentrate on giving and receiving at the same time. So it almost always ends up in some kind of polite turn-taking arrangement, enforcing a passive role for at least half of the time. Once, I faked an orgasm to prompt a lover to stop doing something I didn't like. Yet I learned my lesson. She assumed that was exactly what I wanted next time. So the eventual conversation was more awkward than it need have been.

The few times I did it, I rather liked sex with men. I like goal-oriented sex, the reassuring nature of having a script to follow. I'm a goal-oriented person. Weirdly, sex always felt more equal with men than with women. I like the idea of a position where you can simultaneously thrust towards the same sweaty outcome, maintaining all-important eye contact and maybe kissing or gently biting as you go. I'm not sure if any calorific comparison has been made, but most of the sex I've had with women feels less like a satisfying workout and more like a soothing massage, often with regular tea and snack breaks.

'You can replicate straight sex,' my friend Ali said during a tipsy post-gig group conversation about our frustrations with vanilla lovers, hinting that dildos and toys could be the answer. I groaned, recalling a visit with an ex to Sh! in Shoreditch, an 'erotic emporium' catering for women. But what kind of women are they catering for? Everything is too long and too big. It's like buying jeans in Top Shop. Even though the ridiculous double-ender we left with stayed in its box gathering dust, it had served a purpose in a way. We had giggled like schoolgirls on the bus home, rushing back to have sex for the first time in an age.

My bisexual friend, the former drummer in my band, Lisa chipped in, 'No, no, it's not part of you. You can't feel it.' She was the first person I'd heard expressing the exact same desire I felt for a penis to fuck a woman with.

'I don't want to change anything that's already here,' she said. 'I just want that as well.'

We did a high-five in recognition of our shared frustration.

'The trouble is,' I laughed, 'I'm so good at sex on my own now, I'm not sure if I want to trust my orgasm to some other loser.'

'How often do we all do it DIY?' giggled Lisa.

In unison, we all said, 'Once... every...'

To my amazement, they both said 'Week' as I spluttered, 'Day! Surely?'

'You're pretty highly sexed,' purred Lisa, impressed. I wondered if their working lives perhaps meant they had a lack of opportunity. Ali works in an open-plan office. I guess if she completes a satisfying task, she probably celebrates by making a cuppa and eating a Twix. Whereas I work from home. If I've just booked myself a mini-tour, a little afternoon lie down on the sofa always beckons.

On the Tube home, I googled Sex and Love Addicts Anonymous and toyed with going to a meeting to see if my obsession was becoming a problem. Mind you, I thought to myself, I'd probably just think 'she's hot!' and fall for a fellow addict, thus exacerbating both of our problems.

CHAPTER 11
COUPLES COUNSELLING

As the 159 bus crawled past the late-night hubbub outside Brixton Tube, I began to regret my sauna visit. Still clammy under the shirt and vest I'd hastily thrown back on, I realised that the harder I chased the idea of exciting, fulfilling sex, the more of an abstraction it became. The more I joked about it onstage, the further I pushed it away. Intimacy felt like a distant dream I could only view through a telescope of nostalgia, fractured from my real life in the present.

I undressed downstairs and tiptoed up to the bedroom to slide silently in next to Jen. She was dead to the world, exhausted by another long day and still wearing her crisp work shirt. She was the only woman I knew who seemed to sleep comfortably every night with her bra on. As I closed her laptop and gently manoeuvred it off the bed onto the floor, I felt an overwhelming sense that, if I wanted to rediscover intimacy, it should be with my partner. I trusted her. I knew her. I loved her. Of course it was her. What a dick I'd been to think anything else. I lay as close in as I could without actually touching and waking her, a kind of 'ghost-spooning', my arm burning to extend itself around her waist and hold her.

The next morning I was about to hit the road for a few days on an eccentric rural cabaret tour with a feminist theatre company, work I'd done before and loved. So I knew I only had my regular breakfast chat-time with Jen during which to propose a strategy for reconnection. If I waited, I might change my mind while I was away. I carried out my regimented routine morning tasks on autopilot – making her coffee, my tea, chopping half a banana onto her cereal, half onto mine.

'Umm... so... Can we try couples counselling as a way of really connecting... y'know... properly... sexually?'

Jen was intently reading an email on her work Blackberry. She glanced up at me, with a look of overburdened nausea.

'Ok, yes, but you need to sort it.'

'Of course, yes!' I beamed.

We had a plan. That, at least, felt like something to hold onto.

The old joke goes that three lesbians in a room together are less likely to be indulging in a male-fantasy *ménage-à-trois* than in a spot of couples counselling. Buffeted by sexism and homophobia alongside the everyday stresses and strains of loving and sharing yourself with another human being, many of my gay female peer group had already sought professional relationship advice.

Even I had dabbled previously, this prior experience perhaps not filling me with the greatest confidence. Over a decade ago, I had a few sessions with an ex at what was then London Marriage Guidance. Our slightly frumpy, very straight therapist hadn't been particularly familiar with the peculiarities of lesbian life and love. Added to that, the issue we were there to discuss was my partner's habitual lateness. Naturally, she turned up five minutes from the end of both sessions. We hadn't fixed the problem but I had been granted a valuable chance to speak about my frustrations and come to a place of acceptance that I probably couldn't change her. Which I guess was the point. Tellingly, I have an ongoing happy friendship and business partnership with that particular ex.

It turned out that sneaking off to make furtive phone calls to vet potential sex and relationship therapists while on a tour of remote village halls on the Welsh borders was a pretty challenging process, hampered by poor signal, sound checks, rehearsals and all manner of distractions – not least amending my breakfast order at our B&B from an assumptive 'vegetarian' (they're all feminists, they're bound to be!) to 'full English'. Still, I found a woman I liked the sound of and booked us in.

It wasn't as if Jen and I didn't already know we were polar opposites. I live life on a rollercoaster of highs and lows familiar to any performer or creative. That's the way I am and I've come to love my rollercoaster and understand how to manage and tame it. Yet I've learned, painfully, that being in a relationship with a fellow performer only serves to amplify these peaks and troughs. The resulting high drama, screaming, plate-smashing, door-slamming arguments are a pretty lousy trade-off for the, admittedly, mind-blowing sex.

Jen, however, avoids conflict at all costs and craves peaceful stability. Hearing about her childhood, and particularly her parent's divorce, helped me to understand why.

Our therapist suggested that we must take turns doing dates, sex, intimacy, togetherness one way and then the other. Maybe it's easier to accept that you won't get what you want one weekend if you get to dictate the next. I begged Jen to just sometimes come up with me for the ride in my metaphorical hot-air balloon, even though it is intense, scary, crazy, dangerous and unpredictable. It could also be thrilling, freeing and an escape from work, from the rat race, from the dulling grey consciousness of the real world. She was in tears, not knowing this terrain that I spoke of and this animated version of me. I felt alive and real. Yet I was also in tears as I realised I might as well have been speaking in an alien language. I could do *Jen's* way. I was able to hold back, stifle and suppress. I'd been doing it for years. Yet she couldn't do mine. Because she just didn't *get* it. It was the loneliest conclusion. That was the heart of why we'd designed a relationship with so much space at the centre that it felt like we were barely together.

Which brings us to the thorny issue of...

CHAPTER 12
(IN)COMPATIBILITY

Jen was the first serious partner I had ever met online. Yet I didn't trust it. What I had previously left to magic, luck and good timing now felt manipulated and rushed. If I'd written my profile at two in the morning while crying broken, lonely tears into a tumbler full of neat whisky, chances were that I would attract someone in a similar state. We were on a rebounding collision course of emotional instability, neither of us healed or ready. But new technology has a seductive way of making us believe that it can force love's hand and solve everything.

I'm a great believer in the random, organic nature of meeting in real life. I think of it as a free-range option as opposed to buying my partner from a battery farm. I was always a much happier chicken being too busy and free to be looking for love than I've ever been when I've resorted to searching online. In the early days of internet dating, a decade or more ago, 'available' people were usually the ones still wasting entire evenings taking a deliberately long detour home just so that they could walk past their ex-partner's house and hide behind a bin in order to watch a light going on and off and then draw ridiculously melodramatic conclusions from this paltry information.

Grace Dent recently presented a TV show about modern dating. She met her much younger male partner in a shop. When they set up online profiles as a test, they came up as a zero percent match and would never have come up in one another's searches. They were outside each other's age bracket. They would never have met. Yet when they did a saliva test looking at their relative levels of dopamine, serotonin and oxytocin, and thereby measuring their mutual empathy, they scored very highly.

Dating-app algorithms still seem pretty crude. In terms of matching friendships, they work very well. Shared interests in certain movies and music are a good indicator for successful platonic connection. I have found excellent tennis partners, podcast partners, band members and deep friendships on dating sites. Yet a computer can't yet measure the intricacies and delicate timing of attraction.

Says Qazi, 'the maths is based on a principle of like attracts like. In this sense, the technology comes from behavioural science. But some of the interests and qualities being measured boil down to pretty mundane things like income, education level, IQ, politics, religion, ethnicity (controversially) and personality. Some of these are acting as proxies or windows for other things such as "resources" or "security". It's interesting that we are happy to offload romantic decisions to an algorithm, isn't it? To want to have one's desires directed, and to let go of privacy and some self-control in the process.'

For someone really to catch my eye, I have to meet them just after I've come off stage from a great gig. My brain is awash with happy hormones. I'm in my element. When it goes well, performing *is* sex. For me, it is Puck's magic potion. The first person I see as I say, 'thank you and goodnight,' will be my next crush. There's a hint to anyone who wants to try and make me fall in love with them. Just putting it out there...

Yet even with the steady stream of admirers that a performer's life affords, mathematics still means that it would take a while to find the right one. A BBC Horizon programme *How To Find Love Online* suggested using an Optimal Stopping theory. After rejecting the first thirty-seven of any one hundred potential suitors, it would apparently be easier to make the best possible choice. The next person who seemed just as good as (or even better than) all the discarded options would, presenter Xand Van Tulleken assured me, be *the one*. My average hit rate of sane-ish, attractive women expressing romantic interest has been around one a month for the decade that I've been a comedian. I know! Not bad right? I generally haven't acted upon it, of course, as I've been in relationships. But, in real terms, the equivalent of a minute or so swiping left on Tinder would take me just over three years. If it's a numbers game now, then digital does have the upper hand in terms of sheer volume of possibility.

I still hold onto hope of a real-life chance meeting, however, because I've now reached the very low level of fame at which I have become too famous to do online dating. I am really not famous at all, not enough to be troubled by autograph hunters and TV producers on anything like a regular basis, or to be offered lucrative film roles. The only context in which I'm a household name is if that household is one of the many London lesbian flat-shares I've been thrown out of for inappropriate dalliances with a fellow occupant. I'm not even close to being the UK's most famous actively-gigging lesbian comedian over the age of forty. A tiny niche, surely? But no, I'd have to bump off Susan Calman, Zoe Lyons and several others.

Even so, once Jen and I had admitted and agreed a change in our relationship and I dabbled with an online profile, I was immediately inundated with messages from women who had seen me live. Most had enjoyed it and wanted to know when I was performing again in their neighbourhood. But one seemed quite keen on a critical deconstruction of my set. She still wanted to have a date though. I wondered if she might've gone about it the wrong way. Rather than flirting, I found myself, not only doing gig admin, but defending my jokes. It was deeply unsexy.

I experimented with a slightly ambiguous wording, declaring my primary domestic partnership with Jen but not completely ruling anything out. My emphasis was on authentic lasting connections, platonic or perhaps romantic, that could be simultaneous and support one another, rather than short-lived serial ones that existed in a vacuum. This was interpreted by one woman as seeking multiple sexual partners, something I'm genuinely less interested in than having people to talk to on a deep level. She sent me a mildly aggressive message about 'having my cake and eating it'. I've always found that expression paradoxical. Surely there's no point in having a cake if you have no intention of eating it. When I asked her what her story was, she confessed to 'getting bored every couple of years' and leaving. I didn't say so, but thought she was throwing away a lot of good cake.

If only genuine friend-dating apps existed, that might've been a better option.

My BC (before comedy) experiences of internet dating were not much better. One site recommended my own profile to me. Was it a weird system glitch or a more telling observation, calling out my narcissism? Yet I was still only a seventy-three percent match! One date brought an *X-Factor*-style panel of previous partners along to judge me. I walked out. Sadly my smooth 'I'm better than this!' exit into the pouring rain was marred slightly by the fact that I had left my umbrella under the table and had to nip back to get it.

A friend told me about a suitor who turned up wearing roller-skates so that she could pursue her more quickly down the street after she beat a hasty retreat. I wondered how many people must have walked out on her in order to arrive at this as a *good* tactic.

But surely compatibility, whether calculated by computer, science or a combination of intuition and grown-up negotiation, is right at the nub of the monogamy problem. I can see exactly why it's such a desirable outcome. Who wouldn't want to find their perfect soulmate and have someone to share life with? I get it. For all the anthropological arguments that we're not wired for monogamy, a lot of us seem to want it. But for long-term exclusivity to work seamlessly, you'd need to be nigh-on one hundred percent suited. The glorious, infinite variety of humanity means that this is a very slim chance indeed.

For me to meet my ideal match, I'd need to swoosh two completely different personality types together in a blender. I like experiencing romantic trysts with performers, writers and musicians because I connect with them very deeply emotionally. There's an unspoken mutual understanding about why we do what we do. Yet, aside from a very elite successful minority, most creative types make lousy life partners because they have no money. I've always been resourceful and business-like enough to make a life of creativity pay the bills. I want to live in a nice place and go out to dinner sometimes. But when I have relationships with professional women who can afford to share a more aspirational lifestyle, I feel disconnected and lonely, exiled from my own sexuality and body. As a general rule, if someone can't write a song or a poem, they probably can't press my buttons romantically. It's not that they're bad in bed *per se*. They're just not right for me. They can't understand something that goes deep into the core of my soul, of my identity, the thing that is vital to who I am and why I get up in the mornings. They can't see the problem with having sex to a Keane album as opposed to sophisticated prog-folk like Jonathan Wilson or early John Grant.

Our desires are dictated by what is sometimes known as a 'love map', a template laid down early in our sexual development. Mine rather unhelpfully seemed to have guided me to a pretty perilous T-junction, somewhere between a rock and a hard place, both directions leading to an unhappy, lonely trudge back to the beginning. Go with my sexual instinct and have a passionate yet fractious and difficult relationship, or override it with rational thinking about what is 'good' for me, like yoga or salad (not even a chocolate one). I asked a therapist friend if I could change my template and become attracted to these yoga or salad options. 'No, they're pretty fixed' she said.

It feels particularly counterintuitive as a gay person to go against sexual instinct. One of the greatest decisions we have made, to come out and be our authentic self, is based purely on this 'natural' innate drive. To me, an exclusive commitment to a woman I'm not physically drawn to is the equivalent of settling for a man. It negates something I fought so hard for.

An insight into our own pesky map and suitable 'types' can come from taking a personality test devised by biological anthropologist Dr Helen Fisher. She is a scientific adviser to the site Match.com (the one that sent my own profile back to me) and divides us into four personality categories – director, builder, negotiator and explorer. I completed the test a few years ago and, while I was quite a mix of all four, my main type was 'negotiator', someone who looks at the big picture. The site went on to tell me that an example of this type was Bill Clinton. I would apparently be most compatible with a rational and analytical 'director', an example of which was Hillary Clinton. Clearly, fidelity might be an issue in my future relationships!

There are the lucky few star-crossed couples who might be somewhere up in the ninety-percent compatibility range with neatly intersecting maps and personality types. They're the ones who are probably not posting their every kiss on Facebook. They're secure enough not to *need* to. As I sat around a table in a lesbian bar a couple of years ago with my ex, her more recent ex and other members of a sprawling friendship network, we could think of just one such coupling.

But the rest of us have to try to wrestle with making things work with a much lower matching score. In smaller dating pools, such as lesbian and gay society, certain religious communities, or simply as we get older and everyone around us seems to be partnered up, we can *feel* like we have less choice available to us regardless of whether that's the reality. Having kids from previous relationships, ill health, being bald or short or lacking in confidence or a long list of supposedly 'less attractive' traits can all similarly limit our options.

Liz Bentley says, 'As we get older we are more selective and there may be less to choose from, especially if we have exhausted the local area. It's like having a tin of biscuits. The ones that are left are the broken ones at the bottom.'

Maybe I'm deluded, but I like to think of myself as a biscuit who has fixed herself, covered herself in chocolate and gold foil and catapulted herself back to the top row of the biscuit tin. But still people are suspicious and afraid. Why would that biscuit still be there, pristine, untouched and alone? What's wrong with it?

So we compromise and relent on our absolute deal-breakers. If we want to be in the dating game at all, we face up to a long list of unmet needs, which can lead to resentful martyrdom. Or we need to take a pragmatic approach and find strategies for getting these needs met outside of the primary relationship.

CHAPTER 13
MY BODY IS MY OWN PRIVATE SCIENCE LAB

It was unusual for me to be getting the train home from Edinburgh in May. As I gazed out at the sun-dappled Berwick coastline, I thought about how different the city had been out of Fringe season. Grassmarket and the Royal Mile were almost silent, allowing me the space to daydream. I'd had a fun-filled few days performing a weekend of shows at always-packed comedy club The Stand and my solo show in a peculiar old science lab at Summerhall. A welcoming, fun B&B landlady had been almost constantly on hand with tots of whisky and, more importantly, my own sense of self had been lent some much-needed pizzazz by the blossoming of a new, flirtatious friendship.

Katy and I had connected a few months earlier on Twitter over a shared love of John Grant music and Nordic noir TV shows. I felt a sense of alignment returning, as some of the gaps in my relationship with Jen were starting to be filled by someone else. It was such a relief to feel seen and heard, no longer misunderstood. Here was someone who actively wanted to 'get it' rather than to silence and objectify me as so many others had done, projecting their own ideals onto my hollow shell.

Katy was younger than me, tactile and more open. It felt totally natural to walk hand in hand with her or have our own private jokes and world.

Yet this particular weekend, our online communication had upped several gears to occupy a very murky, grey area. Well aware that 'text and email flirting' had scored highly in my survey as very definitely cheating, I had provocatively sent a photo of my cosy, double B&B bedroom. The subtext was quite clear. 'I wish you were here.'

And so it continued on my journey back towards London, back towards Jen. Yet it wasn't her I was thinking about.

'What would you do if I came straight to you when I got off this train?'

'Kiss you.'

As my phone buzzed excitedly on the fold-down table with Katy's unambiguous response, the ticket inspector appeared at my shoulder and startled me. I felt like I'd been caught red-handed. I was doing something I shouldn't, something I wasn't communicating fully to Jen.

Yet I'd been stifling my sexuality for too long. I didn't like the preachy goody two-shoes I'd become. As the train crossed the Tyne and I craned my neck up to look out for the Angel of the North, I felt myself smiling. My memories of these familiar landmarks were shifting and reforming in my brain. I felt free. The world seemed more colourful and beautiful again.

Spookily, a friend I'd met for coffee just before catching my train up to Scotland had given me an article on romantic friendships that she'd ripped out of *The Times* for me. I fished it out of my bag. In it, psychotherapist Phillip Hodson was saying that: 'Part of the attraction of the romantic friend lies in their potential to rescue or reform your marriage.' Rescuing a marriage honestly by having some needs met outside of it rather than overburdening your partner and then moaning at their inability to be everything at all times sounded like a pretty good idea to me. Yet the article went on to talk about 'warning signs' that your partner is having one of these 'dangerous' friendships. The difference, I thought to myself, surely must be in the intention at the outset of the new relationship. If you're hoping that it will be a catalyst to ending your marriage, then that's a whole different dishonest, passive-aggressive ballgame from hoping that it will make you a happier, nicer, more fulfilled and energised person for your partner to be around... Right?

I switched my attention and focus to texting Jen. When I arrived home, she was in bed working, with her laptop perched on her knee. I spontaneously undressed, got in with her and we had the first sex we'd had in a very long time, and perhaps the most connected we'd ever had.

I expected an inquisition as to where this sudden change in my confidence had come from – but none came. It was perhaps best for us not to question this moment of calm and deep happiness.

There's an old idea that 'women need closeness in order to have sex and men need to have sex in order to feel close'. I'd love to dismiss it as gender-binary, stereotypical twaddle. Yet I have long suspected that I desperately *do* need to feel real emotional intimacy to get anywhere near to rampant horniness with someone. This loosely falls into what is known as a *demisexual* orientation. But what now seemed apparent, in my case at least, was that the closeness might not *have* to be with the person I'm actually having the sex with.

CHAPTER 14
LOVE-AFFAIR FRIENDSHIPS

Over dinner recently, I asked my ex-partner Alice, now a good friend, if she would ever have an open relationship.

'No, no, I don't think I could do that.'

But then after a pause and a smile, she asked, 'but what about love-affair friendships?' She went on to describe an impenetrable fortress of female friendship, her own group of girly best mates who'd known each other since school and had supported and loved each other throughout almost all of their lifetimes. They sounded far more bonded to, and in love with, one another than their respective husbands and partners. While I had clearly muddied my boundaries with Katy and, to some extent, Jen, I knew that this was the sort of intimacy I was really seeking.

It suddenly struck me that we don't have the language to reflect the diversity and breadth of connections we experience. So Alice had empowered herself by making up her own.

Perhaps there is an unexplored grey area in between romantic and platonic love. Yet in this case, grey seems the wrong colour. It is supposedly a shade of neutrality, detachment and compromise. Yet I wonder if a world beyond the oppressive binary of relationships being either sexual or not, might be the richer and more vibrant one after all.

Once I started writing about love-affair friendships, other peers started picking up on the phrase. We abbreviated it to L.A.F. *Telegraph* journalist Rebecca Holman punched the air when I mentioned it in an interview with her. 'I have those friends', she said excitedly, 'but I've never had a word for it.'

The romantic nature of the initial courtship has lifted so very many of my platonic connections way above 'just' friends. It feels actively *more* important, not to be messed up with the random, inconsistent flimsiness of something as ephemeral as sex. In fact, perhaps platonic friendship is the one true, honest and rational love, unclouded by the bizarre chemicals associated with lust that shut down the parts of the frontal cortex associated with critical thinking. We *choose* to laugh, talk, cry and spend time with our friends without needing orgasms to bond us. We love them regardless.

I recently watched Alice get married and promise to

'forsake all others' for her new bride. I couldn't help but glance over to her three 'love-affair friend' bridesmaids and wonder how true that sweeping promise really was. I'm certain that she will do her utmost to remain sexually faithful just as she did in her relationship with me. However, this is a woman who has huge numbers of close romantic connections in her life. Her boundary has always been to allow herself 'love-affair friendships' with heterosexual women only, so that sexual possibility is ruled out from the start. No wonder she has needed to create her own language to navigate this. Without even knowing it, or noticing the irony of using archaic marriage vows, she is a pioneer of a new type of 'currency of commitment'. Even though her wonderful new wife is undoubtedly her number one, other people orbiting around that partnership also have real value.

In my opinion, this is a pretty brilliant strategy for supporting and maintaining a sexually monogamous relationship long term... just so long as your partner isn't one of the seventy-three percent who voted in my survey for 'falling in love' as a form of cheating. Yet, even then, perhaps an exception would be made for pre-existing loving friendships, where the 'falling' part already happened a long time ago.

Although I hadn't heard anyone else devise a new phrase to describe them, intense non-sexual trysts between women are common. 'I would die for them,' says one comedy colleague of her best mates. Another calls them her 'soul sisters', having been bonded together in loyal devotion by the sudden, premature death of one of their gang. Even Facebook, which has rather misappropriated the word 'friend' and diminished its currency, recently suggested that my wonderful platonic pal and emoji-texting buddy Ali is my 'soulmate' in a silly quiz.

The actress Cate Blanchett caused the media to get hot and bothered in 2015 when, during interviews promoting the film *Carol*, she announced that she had had 'relationships' with women. She later explained that these were not sexual. Any woman who had a best friend as a teenager at school knows exactly what she means.

Long before my female peers got boyfriends, and even longer before I bit the bullet and came out, we coupled up. The dynamics of these early relationships played out just like adult romances. There were affairs, dramatic endings, new beginnings, episodes of mate poaching, jealousy, tears, rage and occasional comical catfights behind the gym, all hair-pulling, scratching and slapping. At fifteen years old, I seduced Jo Jones away from her dweeby sidekick Nicola by kneeling at her desk each morning during registration with a handful of Thornton's Alpinis. We were allies in RE lessons because neither of us believed in God. Yet ultimately I was to be usurped by all-too-perfect Head Girl Gillian Appleton. It was devastating. It's the worst feeling of all when you're replaced by someone you actually like. You can't even have the last laugh and think, 'Well, it's her loss if she wants to go round with that *loser*.' However Gillian was a winner. I had unwittingly emboldened Jo to think big and aim for a higher prize than me. We sat together as an awkward threesome in Biology class for a full year pretending that everything was fine. It wasn't. It was in this hothouse of passion that my romantic imprinting occurred. Come to think of it, how does any woman emerge from all that *without* being a little bit gay?

What I didn't realise is that perhaps some of my deep romantic yearnings for my female peers were reciprocated after all. I had interpreted my intoxicating feelings as being 'gay', being different. 'Best-friendship' was a model so fulfilling to me that I didn't want to switch over to men. Yet many straight women seem to maintain both into adulthood. In a 2014 interview in *The Advocate*, Keira Knightley said: 'female friendships are fucking extraordinary. They don't have to be sexual to be intense love affairs.'

Straight women are so lucky. They can have a male sexual partner and a whole separate romantic best friend with whom they can share their most intimate secrets. Straight women are habitually non-monogamous even if they're sexually faithful. My great mistake was to think that I could only attain this romantic intensity with a woman if she was my lover. But the trouble with sex is that it goes off. So if that is underpinning your romantic connection then it automatically lends it an end date, a best-before date. Love becomes conditional. And the condition is sex.

It feels like the relationship is a packet of chocolate biscuits that will be consumed and then just... gone. By being gay and monogamous, I was doubly shooting myself in the foot. I was losing my opportunity to have two separate people at the centre of my life, a lover and a best friend... and I was also having to lose that best friend every few years.

It's the *When Sally Met Sally* phenomenon. Straight girls have girlfriends, as in friends who are fellow girls. Yet if you're both gay, the assumption is that you might as well have a relationship and a sexual element is automatically imposed. So you are only allowed one at a time.

In a recent online chat, comedian Rachel Sambrooks told me that her experience at an all-girls school was so full-on that it was a real relief to have boyfriends. 'As a heterosexual woman, I'm interested in female friendships which are often far deeper than the official relationships I've had,' she said. 'We are given a box to shove our relationships into, which doesn't actually fit the experience.' Whereas her teenage daughter has recently come out and, in Rachel's opinion, 'she hasn't had the intense female friendships because there's so much pressure on it to be something else.'

So maybe I came out for the wrong reasons and I could have indulged in more sapphic romance if I'd actually been straight! Damn! Maybe I had opened myself to a whole load of awkward sexual obligation I never wanted. Really, I was looking for a Thelma to my Louise. I wanted to do girly things, to bitch and moan about period pains and bad bras. Yet most of the women who approached me wore aftershave and wanted to give me a 'backie' on their motorbike. That's all fine and dandy but it's not what I'm searching for.

At the happiest and most authentic time of my life, when I started my comedy adventures, it was no accident that I formed a bond with a fellow stand-up, Jane. Making her laugh felt like walking on air. I adored her. But there was an instinctive trust and respect between us. She was straight and dating men. No awkward conversations were needed to decipher what our friendship was or wasn't and what the boundaries of it were. It was a wonderful feeling to have my love received and understood, without the need for me to squeeze it into unnatural shapes. We met up again for dinner last year and she remarked, 'It's like no time has passed at all,' as we immediately fell back into conversation and laughter just like 'putting on an old pair of favourite slippers'. To me, that's the mark of something real, even if it had begun in the unreal world of stand-up. I sometimes wonder if it was this love that I channelled when I first fell for Sarah, as if Jane had opened up my heart to the possibility of a full relationship. It was the most exquisite hors d'oeuvre – one I didn't ruin by trying to make it into a main course.

Yet women don't always receive one another positively. Despite increased liberalism, the advancement in gay rights, an apparent increase in female sexual fluidity and the over-sharing on social media that we started to see throughout the noughties, I've become more and more aware that we all too readily censor one another's desires. If a friendship is at all one-sided, it seems to be more and more common for the beloved to get totally freaked out and shut the whole thing down.

One of the most popular discussions on my Facebook wall has been about friendship breakups. More than a hundred people, mostly women, have posted real stories of pain that they'd felt they had nowhere to share. In that *The Advocate* interview, Keira Knightley said that 'a breakup with a female friend can be more traumatic than a breakup with a lover.' Yet it isn't recognised by society as anything like the same kind of loss.

Even if we can't always reciprocate, surely it's incredibly flattering to know that someone cares and wants to connect with you? In a 2015 *Guardian* online article on crushes, journalist Nell Frizzell wrote, 'Nobody but a psychopath will be anything but pleased to hear that someone finds them attractive.' Lately I've met a few of these psychopaths, who seemed incredibly angry and offended to be liked. Or perhaps they are just people who had been let down and were fearful of it.

I've always felt a huge sense of responsibility to anyone who has the courage to tell me that they like me. If they can do that, then they're probably worth knowing. These things rarely come about out of the blue. I have probably encouraged their feelings in some way, so I then have to be incredibly careful with them.

Years ago, I decided that the best thing to do is to hang out with them as much as time allows and build a great friendship. Let the relationship evolve and breathe while being clear and consistent about your boundaries. Think about what you *can* offer them rather than focusing on what you can't. If they're still having a fantasy love affair with you in their head, let them enjoy it. It'll be way better than any real relationship and, deep down, they probably know that too. As the years pass, parity of feeling is restored as they get bored and move on romantically. But you have allowed them to move on by allowing them to act out the relationship. If you cut them down right at the start, you leave them stranded in limbo, full of feelings and with nowhere to put them. And you lose the chance of a loving friendship. We need to hear one another and receive one another.

It worked for me and one of my longstanding friends. In fact, I was a little dismayed at just how quickly she went off the idea of a relationship with me. My subtle hints at how terrible I am as a partner were clearly incredibly effective.

Meanwhile, my straight forty-three-year-old comedian and writer friend Heather has her love-affair friendships with men, and keeps them entirely separate from her sexual encounters. 'I've been told on numerous occasions that this makes me well weird,' she says.

119

Declaring herself 'just not built to spend a lot of time around one person' because she always comes to 'hate the sound of their breathing', she has had two key men in her life that she has turned to for 'the things that most women use boyfriends for: emotional support, a man's perspective and getting things off high shelves.' She even bought a house with one of them and lived with him platonically for ten years. He is now happily married – to someone else.

'As I'm not a nun,' she continues, 'I do also have sex "relationships" although to call them that is a bit of a joke. One thing I have noticed though is that, when I was in my twenties and thirties, it worked OK to say "I'm not looking for anything serious". Yet the older you get, the more people seem to think you're just saying that and you're in denial.'

Perhaps as the years tick by, we become more conservative about forming new attachments that don't fit into a reassuringly rigid framework. And the wider world becomes increasingly judgemental about our doing so.

Yet if we constantly have to police our emotions, walk on eggshells, turn our dials down and hold back the tide, dampen the crashing waves within us, then we are not truly living or being ourselves. Mid-life is a vulnerable and lonely time whatever our sexual orientation and family setup. Marriages are at breaking point, aging parents are ill and frail, careers are at stressful junctures and teenage kids are in hormonal overdrive. This is exactly when we need to turn to our love-affair friends, old and new.

CHAPTER 15
BROMANCE AND PLATONIC(ISH) SNOGGING

So much for women's relationships. In the world of men, bromance has enabled them to acknowledge strong platonic affections for one another. My favourite male-bonding movie is the gritty LA police procedural *End Of Watch*. The two lead actors, Jake Gyllenhaal and Michael Peña, have spoken tenderly in interviews about the brotherly love they developed during the shoot. 'He has this amazing heart,' said Gyllenhall, after Peña admitted to having his 'walls' broken down and really being opened up by the friendship.

My friend, the poet Dominic Berry, lives with a heterosexual man and describes their connection as 'a lot like romance. We are very tactile; we cuddle while watching telly; we cook meals together, chat late into the night, are there for each other and go out together. I totally trust him and feel I could ask him anything and he would be there. No-one I have dated has seemed to be jealous of this.'

The American sociologist Eric Anderson holds the position of Professor of Masculinities, Sexualities and Sport at the University of Winchester in England. He suggests that 'cultural homophobia is rapidly decreasing among young men in Anglo-American cultures' and that 'softer and more inclusive masculinities are proliferating'. This 'new' emotional intimacy and tactility between men harks back to ancient Greek times, when male homosocial bonds were culturally prized. What's taken you so long, boys?

Anderson co-authored a 2010 paper on the 'emergence' of heterosexual men kissing. A hundred and forty-five interviews were conducted with young men at universities in the Midlands and south-west of England. Eighty-nine percent had kissed other men on the lips, with thirty-seven percent describing a more sustained mouth-on-mouth contact. This activity was construed as non-sexual and was used entirely as a way of establishing intimacy and friendship.

However, this is all still relatively new in the UK. When I mooted the idea of a platonic snogging revolution in a Facebook thread, one friend posted, 'My young straight male colleague has just choked on his lunch at this concept. Clearly, it has not reached Llandudno yet.' Yet others were more open to the idea. Filmmaker Sebastian Michael commented, 'I grew up, like most boys, thinking that kissing and touching are precursors to sex. So it confused the hell out of me when that wasn't necessarily the case. Some men just like to be close to other men sometimes.' Two lesbian friends described regular platonic intimacy with gay men involving 'cuddling, stroking and non-passionate kissing'. Yet when the activity occurred with female mates, it was much more difficult to leave emotion at the door. There was a higher level of anxiety as to what the significance of the kiss was.

When I lived in a lesbian house-share after my breakup with Alice, I had a snogging relationship with one of my fellow tenants, Nat. One night as I had slightly awkward post-gig casual sex with an audience member called Jenny, Nat burst in with a bottle of Tequila, whipped her top off and asked to join in. Although we laughed this off and she made her excuses and went back to her own room, the damage had been done. I wanted to kiss her.

The next morning, I discovered a note she had pushed under the door in the early hours. It was written in eyeliner. 'You two are gorgeous. Have a lovely night. Sorry if I intruded. But if you want an extra pair of lips, come get me. I have no shame and won't be embarrassed tomorrow.' For some reason, I kept this note for years.

As I gingerly crept downstairs, hungover and sleep-deprived, she was sitting provocatively on the balcony in cut-off shorts and big, vampy sunglasses drinking coffee and making an attempt at creating a pain au chocolat by ripping a baguette in two and shoving a Galaxy inside in a lewd motion. She seemed keen to tell me that she was taking some space from her girlfriend. 'I'm sorry to hear that,' I croaked, fumbling a cup of tea.

She suggested we read to each other from the phone book, to make each other seem boring and non-alluring. Yet as we lingered on the stairs, we were drawn closer and closer together.

For several weeks, we spent hours every afternoon rolling around on my bed, listening to Elvis Costello tapes and locked in fizzy, heady kisses. When our flatmates returned from work each evening, we had secret midnight feasts by torchlight and I listened to her practising the musical score from *The Piano*. I lay next to her keyboard enraptured, a sort of Harvey Keitel to her (less mute) Holly Hunter. She thought that if we always stopped short of removing clothes and touching genitals that it wouldn't count as cheating on her girlfriend. At the time, I thought she was skating on pretty thin ice.

But perhaps if different forms of legitimate intimacy had been discussed back in the early noughties, then we would have been more certain about what we were doing. As it was, her girlfriend seemed to sense something was afoot that she needed to nip in the bud and quadrupled the frequency of her visits. It was only months later, standing in our shared kitchen as she stabbed a fork into a microwaveable meal, that Nat acknowledged how her sudden removal of the world we had created together must have felt like 'losing a limb'. It did. And then some.

CHAPTER 16

ARCHITECT OF MY OWN DOWNFALL

I should have learned my lesson. But by the time summer came around, Katy and I had spent several evenings in full-on snogging sessions. Sneaking down the road to Southwark Playhouse bar after presenting my Tuesday night radio show, we'd settled into a rapturous routine. Once the theatre audience had entered the auditorium, we commandeered a private little corner for a regular canoodle. The semi-public nature of this act not only imposed much-needed boundaries on what we could do, but brought with it just the right amount of risk to make it feel pretty thrilling. Applying the same twisted logic Nat had once done, I thought we were safe so long as we kept our clothes on.

Besides, I wasn't really sure I wanted to go any further than kissing. In all honestly, I didn't particularly miss sex or feel that bothered about it. It was the joyfully intimate act of mouth-on-mouth closeness that I had truly mourned for. And now it was back in my life. It didn't feel so much like cheating as opening up a high-speed route to deep friendship.

It was working pretty damn well for me, enhancing rather than threatening my primary partnership with Jen. 'Other people act as our kindling. Love breeds love. It isn't a finite resource we need to stow away in the attic,' I stated with quite some conviction on a Radio 4 *Four Thought* piece recorded at the ICA, an altogether more lovely experience than Summer Nights had been.

I had compartmentalised par excellence. Yet it was all a little less satisfying for Katy. Acutely aware of the fact that she was single and deserved way more than I could offer, I actively encouraged her to date. I thought that if we both had partners we were committed to long term, we would somehow be more equal and that our ambiguous friendship could carry on as it was. However, what I *actually* wanted was for us to be in the same boat, for her to meet someone and immediately fast-forward four years to a largely-companionate primary relationship alongside which she would still need me for her romantic fix.

So, when her Tinder dates passed by unsuccessfully, a tiny, selfish part of me was relieved every time. What a hypocrite.

We spent the final weekend of my Edinburgh Fringe run together, as she was coming up to write reviews for

Broadway Baby. The promised consummation following our prolonged flirtation turned awkward and slightly sour. I'd had a good month of receptive audiences, buzzing social media activity, pretty decent reviews and hadn't even lost too much money. Yet the dying embers of August always carry with them a whiff of sadness. Constant reminders of the award-winners who've had a life-changing month squash even the most robust comedian's ego, smaller personal accolades and achievements suddenly feeling flimsy and inconsequential. Although I didn't want to be, I was cranky and defensive. I slept on a fold-up bed in the lounge at the tiny, overpriced flat I was renting on Pleasance, leaving her alone in the double.

As we sat opposite one another on the train back to London, I noticed her phone buzz and a smile spread across her face.

'Who's texting?' I asked, innocently.

'Hmmm, there's someone I had a date with last week... and it seems to be going quite well...'

'Oh, that's good,' I beamed, while really thinking, 'Oh shit, this is going to fuck *everything*!'

I'd enjoyed a bit of a sense of having two girlfriends. Yet in that moment, I knew it was probably over.

As we neared home, the train ground to a halt at Potters Bar station, an unscheduled stop.

'We're being held here due to a person on the track.'

The announcement was greeted with weary groans.

My Facebook feed filled up with comedians posting that they were stuck on the same train and on the one behind it.

The savviest performers leapt out for the few available taxis, Sue Perkins among them, hot-footing it from First Class. Katy and I stayed restlessly and passively in our seats, wondering how long the delay would be.

After about half an hour, I was so tired I couldn't bear it any longer. I phoned ever-reliable Jen.

'I'm stuck at Potters Bar. Is there any chance you'd drive up and get me? ... Oh, and maybe you could drop my friend Katy at the Tube, too?'

Every time I referenced Katy, I included the prefix 'my friend' as if to reinforce the innocent, platonic nature of our connection. It was so ridiculously obvious that something was off. And here I was putting her and Jen in a car together. What was I thinking? I had almost had a full-blown affair. Yet was kidding myself it was nothing.

As Jen pulled up, I glanced at the stationary train above us on the bridge and hoped I'd done the right thing. We made polite conversation as my addled mind, still high from the narcotic fuzz afforded by performing several times a day for weeks, tried to come to terms with this unplanned meeting between my two separate romantic worlds.

'Which Tube do you need?'

'Oh really, just any you're passing... It's fine'

'Did you see any good shows?'

'Loads of theatre stuff, not so much comedy... Oh, you

could drop me here if that works...'

I got out of the car to retrieve her bags from the boot, hugged her... and then she was gone.

CHAPTER 17

WHAT DO WOMEN WANT?

THANK GOD THERE'S A MAN AROUND TO TELL US!

Perhaps aware of her role in my own private science experiment, Katy's rather knowing parting gift was a copy of a book by *New York Times* journalist Daniel Bergner. In *What Do Women Want?*, he gathers evidence of a kind of existential despair felt by women in long-term, monogamous, mostly straight relationships. He suggests that the craving for sexual and romantic novelty is much more vast and profound in women than in men, something that we have not previously admitted or explored.

While reading it, I immediately started to wonder if all-too-often-overlooked lesbian relationships could hint at some universal answers. We are the ones who hold vital intelligence about what women get up to in relationships with no men around to muddy the picture. Perhaps we reveal something about what *all* women actually *want* and how straight women might behave if they could. We are a unique control group. We are an oestrogen-stuffed Petri dish of synchronised menstrual cycles. We are woman-squared.

Anyone who's ever watched an episode of *The Apprentice* will think that, when women are left to our own devices, we are reduced to squabbling and cat-fighting. Yet gay women over the past few decades have devised all kinds of strategies for compassionately coping with the peculiarities of female-female relationships.

Paradoxically, secrecy had some good side-effects. In a small clandestine community, you couldn't afford to be a dick. It's only really being messed up now that we are adopting marriage and normative structures without a clear understanding of how they could be adapted to work best for us and our unique circumstances. We risk losing important information about instinctive female behaviour, not to mention some fabulous stories, as old-school lesbians begin to die out...

Time for my inner geek to come out and revel in some stats. (Stick with me...)

The UK Office of National Statistics (ONS) released figures in 2011 showing that the majority of hetero divorces were initiated by women. It was sixty-six percent of cases that year. Although down on a whopping seventy-two percent at the start of the 1990s, it's still a fairly hefty suggestion that women are more likely to call time on a relationship. Men may well get up to all kinds of things (leaving toilet seats up, forgetting anniversaries and secretly giving themselves the best portion of food – yes, a few admitted this in my survey!). *But* they don't tend to walk away.

A logical extension to draw from this would be that lesbian relationships would be the most likely to break down. This appears to be true, evidenced by 2013 ONS figures showing civil partnership dissolution rates which are twice as high for female couples as they are for male unions. When writer and activist Peter McGraith was researching 2016 Radio 4 documentary *For Better Or Worse*, he made a Freedom of Information request for early same-sex divorce statistics in the UK. What he found was that the trend had actually increased. 'For every gay male couple that filed a divorce petition, 3.2 female couples did so,' he said in his accompanying BBC online article.

Even in countries where same-sex marriage has been around for longer and figures might be expected to have settled down, the ratio is still double. In a 2013 Central Bureau of Statistics survey in The Netherlands, where marriage equality became law in 2001, just fifteen percent of male-male couples had divorced, as opposed to thirty percent of female-female. These figures are still below the divorce rate for all couples of 36.3 percent.

However, statisticians tend to guesstimate that the average same-sex divorce rate is probably roughly equivalent to the heterosexual one, once the shorter exposure time to marriage is accounted for. In other words, we will catch up. And, if the *average* rate catches up, then this will probably mean that lesbians leapfrog straight couples to the top of the divorce charts. While gay men sit snugly, or perhaps smugly, below us all.

When I mentioned these stats on BBC *Woman's Hour*, presenter Jane Garvey asked her producer to check them. I promise – I wouldn't make this stuff up! It's not really in my interests to suggest that lesbians aren't doing so well at this commitment lark. I want to empower myself by understanding what's happening.

Bergner isn't the only writer to argue that many women have to engage in some kind of disconnect with the vastness of their own sexuality in order to stay faithful long term. In her book *Vagina*, Naomi Wolf suggested that, for a woman, having sex with someone who has come to feel like the 'wrong' partner can erode her very sense of self. The most recent NATSAL (National Survey of Sexual Attitudes and Lifestyles) findings reported that women were twice as likely as men to say that a lack of interest in sex had been an issue within the last year. No wonder, then, that lesbian couples are doubly hit by these challenges.

Sociologist Pepper Schwartz coined the term 'lesbian bed death' in her 1983 book *American Couples* after finding that gay women reported the lowest frequency of sexual activity in longer-term relationships. Her survey has attracted criticism from some modern lesbians who argue that the couples might have been confused by what counted as 'sex'. However, I think we tend to know in our souls when we have had sex and are rarely seeking to wriggle out of it by way of pedantic Bill Clinton-esque definitions. When I googled the phrase 'lesbian bed death', I found a rock band using this unlikely moniker. One of their songs has the insightful title, 'She Wants It (Just Not With You)'!

Interestingly, a new female 'Viagra' turns out to work like an anti-depressant. A recent TV news item about it included a clip of a woman saying she 'just wanted to desire her husband again'. Tellingly, she didn't say she wanted to 'feel desire again' per se. Perhaps the real challenge was in desiring the person she was married to. Experiments in labs on female rats have shown them rapidly go off sex with a familiar partner but utterly re-energised by a new one. Whereas divorced heterosexual male friends tell me they were still in love with their wives and would happily have been faithful, loving and constant. Yet they were kept at arm's length for years before being dumped.

So not only are women more likely to go off a partner, they also seem to prefer to leave a relationship altogether rather than look outside of it for fulfilment of unmet needs as a strategy for staying put. While this may be a noble intention, it is arguably more disruptive to the ecology of our wider family and friendship networks.

Many gay men successfully negotiate an open relationship yet stay *emotionally* faithful to one partner, hence their lower separation rates. A San Francisco study found that, in 2000, reported sexual activity outside a relationship was down to eight percent among gay women and fifty-nine percent for gay men after much higher stats across the board in the 1970s. For reference, heterosexual men and women were at ten and fourteen percent respectively.

Other studies in the 1980s suggested that fifty-three percent of gay male couples and just four percent of lesbian partnerships had consensual non-monogamy agreements in place. Even my own modest survey suggested that lesbians were having the fewest affairs, thereby trying the hardest at monogamy, yet had by far the highest number of serious, serial partners.

Qazi Rahman explains that women tend to have a lower socio-sexual orientation – a willingness to engage in sexual activity outside a committed relationship. Whereas men tend to be more sensation-seeking. 'But,' he says, 'some of that sex difference is affected by social factors like gender equality and economic development.'

So if gay women do want to have sex (yes, please!) but are not finding it possible either inside *or* outside their longer-term relationships, the only solution in a monogamous society is to break up.

Yet what strikes me is that gay men and lesbians in previous decades had arrived at open relationships and serial monogamy respectively as fairly savvy and self-aware strategies for solving the thorny issue of long-term fidelity. Perhaps these clear patterns of behaviour emerged because that was exactly what suited men and women best. This 'light-bulb' moment occurred as I read Jasper Rees' review on *The Arts Desk* website of the turgid TV documentary *The Secret World of Tinder*. He asserted that it was 'an anthropological film about addiction – to romance for the women, to sex for the men.' If it's not too reductive to assume that these really are our gendered priorities, then of course women would prefer periodically to rotate partners. Once the initial dopamine-fuelled romantic phase is over, then we seek out our next fix.

As the song goes, 'Love is the drug'. In a 2008 TED Talk, biological anthropologist Helen Fisher spoke about an experiment she conducted where she scanned the brains of students who described themselves as 'madly in love'. The resulting images were lit up with activity in the brain's reward centre. Fisher said at the time, 'It's part of what we call the reptilian core of the brain, associated with wanting, with motivation, with focus and with craving. In fact, the same brain region becomes active when you feel the rush of cocaine.'

Given its parallels with romantic love, it's not a surprise to read in Patricia A. Broderick's 2014 paper that females have a higher sensitivity to the effects of cocaine and are more vulnerable to addiction. The sex difference may be explained by the fact that the drug disrupts a woman's oestrus cycle. I wonder if women would be better at staying faithful for longer with one partner if we were actually given cocaine. Now there's an experiment that wouldn't have too much trouble attracting volunteers.

While gay men appear to have got the better deal, and lesbians have to go through several traumatic and expensive separations in a lifetime in order to feed our habit, serial monogamy only becomes really problematic when lifelong monogamy is the *expectation*.

In previous decades, lesbians were living out romantic lives that, while difficult and secret, also felt new, radical and thrilling. They didn't seek to emulate straight couples by breaking into nuclear units and having kids. Clandestine social gatherings were held in women's homes rather than in bars and public spaces. Community was everything. Small networks, coupled with rejection by biological relatives, prompted them to cultivate a concept of 'friends as family' and to retain strong links with ex-partners rather than cut off. Seen through this lens, serial monogamy could be seen as advantageous, a way to build a larger pool of emotional connections. The more caring exes you had, the more people you had to call on when you needed a 'soul sister'.

In her 1988 book *Unbroken Ties*, Carol Becker studied lesbian ex-lovers in San Francisco and suggested that they were 'an important source of validation for each other', the continued connection working to assert a sense of identity in the face of prejudice.

I spoke to Dr Jane Traies, who recently conducted the first comprehensive survey of older lesbians in the UK, collecting anecdotes and data from four-hundred women in their sixties and beyond. 'It's not uncommon,' she said, 'for a lesbian's ex-partner to be her best friend.' Often the ex becomes close to the new partner too. Traies described a couple, now in their seventies, one of whom had previously been in a straight marriage. The other had always been gay and had many more exes, of whom four or five were significant. They would regularly visit them, house-sit and cat-sit for them. The central relationship seemed to be richly rewarded by having this framework of other ongoing connections supporting it.

One woman even said that the best way to make a really good friend was to have a brief relationship, as if the sexual intimacy, while short-lived, had cemented a deeper bond to take forward. Yet these principles of community building are rapidly vanishing...

CHAPTER 18

THE MAGICALLY DISAPPEARING GAY

Some equality campaigners would argue that in a more tolerant, progressive era, in the Western world at least, we no longer need to live in a separatist gay ghetto. Now we can adopt a nuclear family model, why would we maintain what the writer Armistead Maupin refers to as 'logical family'? Why would we congregate *en masse* when we can, largely, mingle and wander safely in mainstream, straight society?

This dampened urgency of the queer agenda has resulted in the closure of historic LGBT venues in major cities across the Western world. In London, a battle rages over the future of the Royal Vauxhall Tavern, a place so imbued with legend that Princess Diana wanted to check it out and once encouraged Freddie Mercury to smuggle her in disguised as a male model in army jacket, cap and sunglasses. A recent multimedia installation at the BFI by artist Allyson Mitchell took the form of a 'lesbian haunted house'. Eerie cobweb-covered gravestones bore the names of long-defunct yet sorely missed clubs, bookshops and cafés. It was a striking metaphor for the slow, crumbling death of an exciting, alternative world I had once aspired to be at the heart of. I hear similar stories from Manchester, New York and Los Angeles.

These centres of gay life were so much more than bricks and mortar, than mere drinking dens. For so many of us, they were our home. Writer Ben Walters describes them as a 'lifeline', representing 'decades of experience, connection, memory and knowledge'.

Peter McGraith asks, 'Do we care if marriage equality contributes to the demise of gay culture, identity and community?' and then resoundingly answers, 'I do!'

Remarkable and laudable as recent political advances have been, they have, paradoxically, exacerbated one particular gay romantic dilemma – scarcity. However equal we are, we are still a teeny tiny minority group in cold, hard numbers. Even Kinsey's estimate, back in the 1950s, that one in ten were homosexual seems generous in comparison to 2013 ONS figures suggesting that 1.1 percent of UK adults were gay or lesbian and 0.4 percent bisexual. So, isolated young gay people have always flocked to the big cities to seek one another out. Overnight, you could be catapulted from an existence as the 'only gay in the village' to the bustling, concentrated queerness of Soho or Canal

Street. Yet if these areas are, quite literally, 'straightened out' and our venues are bought up by property developers, demolished and turned into luxury flats, an exhilarating sense of sexual possibility is immediately diluted. What's the point of being able to marry if there's no longer anywhere to go and meet someone *to* marry?

In the mid-1990s, I regularly attended legendary lesbian mega-club Venus Rising at The Fridge in Brixton. Women of all classes, backgrounds, skin colours, shapes and sizes queued around the block to dance, flirt and laugh into the early hours. Sister Sledge's 'We Are Family' was an unofficial theme tune. It meant everything to feel such a strong sense of belonging and, if you were looking for love, a sense of having choices. And if you have a choice, you can make a better one.

At a recent 'Queer'd Science' symposium at the BFI, Qazi Rahman was speaking about the biology that plays a role in determining our sexual orientation. Rebutting a common fear that this knowledge could be used to filter out or 'cure' homosexuality, he provocatively and playfully suggested that we could do the exact opposite and positively select it as a trait. We could make more gay people! Of course, I don't see this actually happening. But, unless it does, we need to retain some form of selective, separatist socialising in order to connect, then fall in love, and either be monogamous or not.

The scene wasn't *only* about drinking and partying. There

were gay choirs, theatre companies, campaign groups and sports clubs. Even I sometimes wondered if separatism had gone mad as I sat sipping tea from a mug emblazoned with a gay slogan, discussing a book by a gay author with other gay people at a gay book group in a gay café. The zenith was surely reached when I was handed a business card by a lesbian locksmith. As supportive as I am of community endeavour, I've never stopped in that awful moment as the front door slams behind me and I realise I've locked myself out to think to myself, 'Only a *lesbian* locksmith will do!' But... what if the lesbian locksmith was gorgeous? If I already knew she was gay, I'd be able to suggest coyly that I might lock myself out again sometime so that she could come back. Maybe she would turn out to be the love of my life. None of that would happen if I phoned Keys 4 U.

These memories all sound rather quaint now. But the point is that being oppressed had the rather *good* side effect of making gay people more tolerant of, and kind to, one another in the face of a common enemy. This 'bogeyman' was largely embodied by the Tory government with their homophobic policies. Following on from the lesbian collective I'd met at university, 1990s queer London subculture was the place where I truly learned about love and friendship. Perhaps the leftie, activist, artsy groups I sought out already had a bias towards a sense of collectivism and collaboration. Yet the reality of my experience is that gay people were less selfish then.

Perhaps *all* people were nicer in the days before social media. But narcissism and individualism has accelerated all the more quickly within the gay and lesbian community precisely because we were previously more cocooned from it in our own bubble. One symptom of equality is that now we can be as nasty as everyone else.

There was once a precious and powerful intimacy about saying 'I'm gay' to a fellow queer. I even know one gay man and lesbian who found their mutual coming out so connecting that they ended up sleeping together. Now this sense of specialness is lost. Nobody cares if you're gay. This should be a progressive thing. However it feels anything but.

The systematic dismantling of my community has caused me just as much grief and trauma as any of my own romantic breakups. And this sadness has certainly played a role in my insecurities within my personal relationships. If something so meaningful can be whisked away so easily, then what is there to believe in?

Even in a more fluid contemporary climate, with young people abandoning fixed labels, most default to a kind of hetero-flexible identity. *Significant* relationships are with the opposite sex, even where same-sex experimentation and dabbling increases. Legitimising same-sex relationships feels like the very thing that has kick-started the process of their extinction. The surveys indicate a decrease in numbers of 'gay' people precisely because there's less of a political necessity to wear the badge with pride. It is the ultimate paradox.

Gay women in our forties are the generation at the apex of this complex tipping point. The old-school way, the future I had planned, has tumbled and crumbled away. The community that I had grafted my way towards the centre of has dissolved in front of my eyes. Once-sturdy pillars of knowledge and certainty cascade in an avalanche down the hillsides of my mind, my sense of purpose neutered, my identity stolen.

For me and my peers, the new way of broader, more relaxed identities and nuclear families has come just a little too late. Our biological clocks have ticked past having babies and the partners we might have married are long gone. We have fallen down a mountain crevasse into a lonely void, our rainbow cheers and chants silenced by this strange new snowfall that they call 'equality'. Where labels become meaningless, then so do we.

It is under these circumstances that I feel forced to re-evaluate my take on commitment and fidelity. I had mentally chalked up a list of 'lesbian rules' in my mind, handed down to me by older women I adored and admired. Yet someone came along and erased everything.

CHAPTER 19
THE RECIPROCITY PARADOX

Here's a typical conversation between two gay women:

Woman A: I fancy you.

Woman B: Oh, that's amazing... because... I fancy you too.

Woman A: Shit, now you've ruined it.

I have alternated roles in this conversation ad nauseam. This was not part of an acting class. This has been my real life. I feel like a science-fiction character stuck in a time loop, powerless to change the outcome. She dumps me or I dump her. Flip-flop, flip-flop, flip-flop... ricocheting from suffocat*ing* to suffocat*ed*, we feed the serial-monogamy monster.

There's a well-known visual gag comparing how to turn on a man and how to arouse a woman. The man has one basic on-off switch. The woman has a labyrinthine dashboard, a vast array of sophisticated dials. Although, once again, there's a whiff of gender-binary bullshit here, there *is* a truth that women are, largely speaking, more damn complex. Men want to have sex. Women want to have the right type of sex, with the right person, at the right time, in the right room, with the right music playing, with the right lighting, with the right, perfect bloody *everything*. Just imagine how hellishly unlikely it is that two people in a partnership will synchronise when they are *both* dependent on such a huge set of variables. In other words, when they are both women. It's like finding the intricate combination to a safe... twice over. Typically, one has to jettison her desires and sacrifice herself.

Perhaps because many of our early sexual templates were formed around unrequited straight crushes, a lot of lesbians I know do seem much happier in the reassuringly familiar, active role of desiring than in the seemingly more passive, claustrophobic role of being desired. Agreeing to go out with someone on their terms often feels like an act of surrender. We have become so adept at projecting our own agenda onto the object of our desire, that we often no longer see her at all. In my show, The Science Of Sex, I illustrated this disconnect by drawing a Venn diagram on my flip chart. The two circles, 'people who fancy me' and 'people I fancy', barely intersected at all.

It's not, of course, an exclusively lesbian problem. Jung once described the dangers of couples of becoming 'container' and 'contained' and, I'm sure, was largely referring to heterosexual pairings. But the number of one-sided romantic entanglements and one-sided separations I've witnessed within my friendship group makes me wonder if lesbians, in particular, struggle around these sort of power dynamics. In the early twentieth century, European gay women often settled into clearly-defined butch and femme roles as a way round this. But now we are all feminists and falling back on old gender stereotypes doesn't seem right. Besides, I'm a femme who fancies other femmes. So a thorny question emerges... Who asks who out?

Certainly, I've found that women who declare undying love for me have a habit of popping up at the wrong time for me to be in the right place to return their feelings. When I'm not over someone else, when I've just been drenched by a passing bus careering through a dirty puddle, or when I've just emerged from the dentist with a frozen mouth. Seeking out reciprocal attraction has mostly been as futile as panning for gold in the River Thames. It's that old adage that you're more attractive when you're not looking so you have to desperately pretend not to be looking while you actually are. Because if you're really not looking, then you don't notice the people who are interested and they give up.

Pretty much every gay woman I've spoken to about this whole dynamic conundrum craves to be the initiator, the hunter as opposed to the prey. The hunter is always the one left heartbroken when the prey retreats as a last resort, their only way of gaining control. Not only are women turned on by playing out a dramatic romantic story, they want to be the one to write it.

Bearing all this in mind, I wonder if a utopian poly structure for lesbians would be to have 'one of each'. If sexual attraction is never equally reciprocal, then would we be happier and more fulfilled if we were part of a perfect infinite chain of desire? In other words, if we had one lover who desires us and gives us security... and one that we fancy who gives us hope and excitement. They in turn would have another person that they pursue and provide security for. And so it goes on and on. Would this be a way to avoid being trapped in either one binary role or the other?

Much of my romantic imprinting occurred while watching the 1980s American TV show *Moonlighting* on a tiny black and white portable TV in my bedroom. In my head, my romantic alter ego was a young, fluffy-haired Bruce Willis. If I could be charming, witty and solve a mystery now and then, maybe I would find, and ultimately win, my Cybill Shepherd. It felt like Bruce was the hunter, the chaser, the pursuer, the active one. So I had to project onto him, the male role.

Yet I'm not male. I want to live in a world where I'm allowed to express myself as a sexual woman and fall in love with women, and where there are role models and narratives to follow. As a performer, I know how reassuring it can be to have a script to fall back on. Only then can we feel safe to ad-lib and experiment.

When I went out with men, I had both a script and the upper hand dynamically. It was easy-peasy to fool them into thinking they were in charge when actually I was. Everyone wins. But there's no way of pulling the wool over a fellow woman's eyes. They're too damn perceptive. And so a power struggle ensues, a destructive dance of death. If both parties survive, they're simply too exhausted to have sex. Now *that's* the real reason for lesbian bed death.

Admitting that women sometimes behave badly and hurt one another has been a bitter conclusion for me to come to. It's like realising that Father Christmas doesn't exist (sorry guys) or biting into a delicious chocolate bar only to find that it is filled with Brussels sprouts. I entered my sapphic existence totally blinkered by feminist idealism. Expecting to arrive in a utopia where women acted in an emotionally superior way to men has been unhelpful. It left me exposed to deceit and heartache. Sometimes women lie to, cheat on, manipulate, blackmail, bully, threaten and sexually or physically attack one another. Accepting this (I'm still not sure I completely have) will no doubt help me truly and more fully to appreciate the really cool and fabulous women who do amazing, lovely things for me and for others.

How can we have better female-female relationships unless we accept that women are just as flawed as everyone else?

CHAPTER 20

SEX PARTIES AND SNOGGING MEN

I was beginning to feel so despondent about lesbian relationships that I wondered if I was really gay at all. Yet that was a pretty big, scary question to be asking. My sexual orientation had informed every facet of my life, every comedy show I'd written and every major decision I'd made about where I wanted to live, who my friends were and where I hung out. If I wasn't a lesbian, then who the hell was I?

I wrote a pitch for a new comedy show entitled 'The year I dated men to try to get the woman of my dreams'. My warped logic was that a femme-fatale-free calendar year would remove me from the sugar-high boom and bust cycle of my addiction to the intensity of woman-on-woman trysts. Connecting with men again, I thought, might teach me something. One of my biggest regrets at cocooning myself in a lesbian-feminist bubble for years had been losing touch with straight men. It was only starting comedy in my thirties that put me back in touch with the idea of making male friends, when it became an essential survival tactic as there were so few women around.

I pondered whether I could really go back to actual sex with men, sex with a penis. Those experiences were so long ago, back in my student days, that really my partners had been boys rather than men. I wondered how much all those penises had grown in the meantime. Maybe they were all, like, totally eye-wateringly huge now. I had no idea.

And what would happen if I fell for a man? Would I be expelled from my social set, cast out of my lesbian life? Look at what happened to 'hasbian' Jackie Clune, who I once sang with in a queer choir. Once she hooked up with a man, her body started chucking out babies like there was no tomorrow. Would I similarly go into mumsy overdrive at the mere whiff of some sperm? I hoped not. Being a parent wouldn't fit with my manic, nocturnal lifestyle at all. I felt about as maternal as Karen Matthews, a woman who faked her own daughter's disappearance for money.

I applied for an Edinburgh slot for the show. Several male comedy promoters replied enthusiastically, not only at the potential hilarity and marketability of the idea, but vociferously volunteering to be a part of my experiment. My kinky lab rats were keen, to say the least. Reader, I went off this show idea and wrote something else instead.

Still, a new openness about my potential sexual fluidity added to my excitement as I sat on the Overground to Shoreditch one sunny September Saturday evening. I was booked to perform a short comedy set at Kinky Salon, the sort of event my younger self would never have known about and certainly wouldn't have dared to attend. Although I'd heard via the sex-positive community grapevine that this was one of the fluffiest and friendliest of orgies, it was still essentially a sex party. People were going there to fuck. As part of the cabaret that would precede the opening of a discreetly curtained-off 'playroom', I would be their foreplay. A prospect I was relishing. I'd never played to an audience high on pheromones before. Naturally, I'd be keeping things short and punchy.

The fancy-dress theme was, fortunately, 'science'. I wasn't the best fancy dresser but I could just about pull off a sexy science researcher with lab coat, safety goggles and a few props from my Science Of Sex show. I opted for hot pants, sheer tights and knee-high boots under the lab coat, a look I still more or less had the figure to get away with.

A sense of mutual respect and accountability within the Kinky Salon community seemed largely to stem from a 'pal' system. Nobody can enter the party events without another person who will vouch for their behaviour and take them home if they get drunk, rowdy or pushy. I had been racking my brains in a panic, wondering which of my friends I could take.

'It's not my thing at all,' said Jen, dismissively.

I longed for her to shrug off her misgivings and come with me. It's not that I would ever have the audacity actually to have sex among a throbbing, grinding group of people. But I quite fancied the idea of getting high on the hedonistic atmosphere together and then going home to have wild, exclusive sex with my partner.

I toyed with asking exceedingly flirtatious friend Lisa but then wondered if I felt I *could* vouch for her behaviour. Over the years, she had inadvertently broken the hearts of several of my best friends. That was just her way.

Fortunately, one of the event's crew I knew a little agreed to be my pal and I was free of my normal, daily life and relationships and able to reinvent myself for the evening. I skipped down the secret side street and past the security man. An absurdly orderly queue was briefed on the rules. *Do* negotiate your boundaries, play safely and consensually, practise safer sex, respect the space and each other, clean up after yourself. *Don't* assume, cruise aggressively, enter the playroom solo, get too intoxicated or take photos. There seemed to me to be quite a few useful take-home messages for everyday relationships, let alone just for the event.

As I entered, the feel-good factor hit me like a jubilant wall. I noted how little people were drinking and how well they were communicating their desires. I struck up conversation with a couple. They seemed relatively soberly dressed, I thought, until he asked me to hold his girlfriend's lead while he popped to the loo. I limply yet obediently took it from him and awkwardly looped the leather around my hand.

'How did you two meet?' I was really thinking, 'Oh god, what if they think I want a threesome.'

'Oh, I've been looking for someone to dominate me for ages,' she chirruped.

I smiled anxiously, glancing discreetly over her shoulder in the direction of the toilets and wondering how long he'd be.

'Have you tried Shibari?' she asked.

Thinking it sounded like some kind of relaxing meditation, I spontaneously said, 'No, but that sounds divine.'

Later on, I googled Shibari. It turned out to be a type of Japanese rope bondage.

Just as he arrived back with drinks (bloody hell, he took time out to go to the bar *as well*) and I enthusiastically handed back my temporary and wholly unconvincing 'dom' status, the start of the cabaret was called by the MC.

I couldn't have enjoyed myself more onstage had I been having multi-orgasmic sex up there. I felt hilarious and more than a little bit desirable. I was totally rocking the sexy scientist look. The audience were up for it, in every sense.

My plan had been to run for the night bus once I'd come offstage but I turned back, distracted by an amorouslyentwined foursome blocking my exit. There's always just the right amount of time to loiter after a gig. Too brief and you miss out on the reassuring glow of positive feedback. Too long and you look desperate, like you're waiting for something. This was doubly the case on this occasion.

A smiley man dressed as a faun with bare, toned chest, furry legs and tail strolled over to tell me that he found intelligent, funny women attractive. As I'd proclaimed my lesbianism onstage, I sensed that there were no real expectations on his part. Yet as I cast my eye across the room to see endless cuddling straight couples, I thought, 'Ah well, when in Rome...'

I recalled how a few nights earlier, New York comic Lewis Schaffer had attempted to engage me in some verbal jousting, as he often does, by enquiring what percent lesbian I was. 'To you, Lewis', I'd smiled, 'one hundred percent.' Tonight there was just a tiny bit more room for manoeuvre.

Standing fairly publicly in the main bar area, we kissed and chatted for about half an hour, pondering how well or not his costume fitted the theme. It was all a little like snogging one of my platonic female friends... safe and cosy, as opposed to romantic and lusty. A long-disused synapse in my brain had forgotten how to fire at the scent and feel of a man. The empathy in the room was so great that he knew we wouldn't go any further than kiss without needing to explicitly discuss it. I gave him an affectionate squeeze and said, 'Now, go and have a *great* night.'

I legged it for the last bus back to south London, high as a kite, and more present, alive and connected to my body than I had been in a long, long time.

CHAPTER 21
MEN SQUARED

In much the same way that lesbians hint at some universal truths about women, so gay men provide a fascinating insight into instinctive male behaviour. They reveal something about what all *men* want and how straight men might behave if they could. What I really needed to do to immerse myself in a bit of testosterone-packed action would be to hang out with the gay boys.

Dominic Berry points at the fact that being gay in the first place provides an alternative framework for thinking about relationships. 'Perhaps if people are doing something so widely viewed as deviant, making another deviance from the norm isn't too big a jump.'

When I asked my friend and fellow performer Nick Field about the prevalence of open relationships within the queer male community, he could only think of one long-term couple he knew who didn't have such an arrangement. Given gay men's low divorce rate, the pragmatist in me is pretty convinced by this seemingly brilliant model. American sex columnist Dan Savage says, 'Every gay male couple I know in a serious and successful long-term relationship is non-monogamous, even the ones who were monogamous the first ten years.' One of my gay male survey respondents said, 'My partner and I don't have sex very often but we are very lovey-dovey, tactile and romantic. I have sexual satisfaction from other people and the Internet.'

I get it. Why break up a great team and go through all the upheaval we lesbians were periodically subjecting ourselves to for something as simple and available as sex? And boy, any glance at the sex-focused ads in the free gay boys' mags makes it feel like it's pretty available.

My occasional radio co-host, the DJ and writer Stewart Who, has long-term female platonic friends whom he talks to for hours every day. These are his love relationships through which his emotional needs are met. Yet he likes his sexual partners to turn up, have sex and then leave 'before the sweat cools on my body'. Some of these lovers become regular partners for many years. Yet if any of them ever suggest going to an exhibition or social event together, he can immediately sense his desire wilting.

As I found myself being ridiculously turned on by the twenty-minute opening scene of French film *Theo and Hugo*, I felt a pang of envy at gay men's apparent freedom and ease around their most animal instincts. I had always found it a struggle even to admit to a partner what really got me going. Surely gay men were the ones who were being honest about their basic needs and, on some level, had got it right.

A survey carried out in February 2016 by *FS Magazine* and health charity GMFA found that forty-one percent of their sample of 1006 UK-based men had experienced, or were in, an open relationship. Of those, three-quarters believed it to be a 'great' relationship model. However twenty-one percent admitted to breaking the rules they and their partner had agreed.

After recording my Radio 4 piece on marriage with Peter McGraith, we struck up a lengthy correspondence on non-monogamy. If something as perfunctory as an email can ring with delight, his certainly did when he informed me, 'I have a wonderful, life-enhancing, horny, multi-ethnic coterie of regulars, occasional and one-off fucks as well as my gorgeous **** of a partner.'

He talked me through four typical styles of gay male open relationships.

'All out in the open – Both are able to discuss what each gets up to, even to the extent that they'll meet other guys at the same time in different rooms of their house; or one will use the bedroom with a fuckbuddy while the other gets on with his work in the study. Or they might attend sex parties together while also pursuing sex with other guys separately

through online cruising. Guys in this type of relationship may tell their friends, workmates and relatives about their non-monogamy, or in certain instances might provide each other with alibis to help deal with prurient interest. This setup allows partners more space to be honest about any sexual infections that they pick up, rather than sexual health being an each-man-for-himself issue.

Don't ask, don't tell – There is some kind of understanding that each person is allowed their own private life. Each agrees to turn a blind eye in return for having their own freedom. There might be some minimal negotiation, such as agreeing only to see other guys when one or other is out of town. What happens in Vegas stays in Vegas. Guys might also have the odd threesome together. Although it can be a very trusting setup, it can be the case that one partner worries that he's not having as much sex outside of the relationship as his partner.

Only play together – Online profiles of lots of coupled guys declare that they stick to this rule. However, from my experience, it seems like a way for some couples to deflect criticisms of disunity. Is this a way to operate an open relationship without labelling it as such? In some cases OPT couples may become cruising buddies, possibly because they particularly get off on sharing/seeing their partner with another guy or, for example, because both realise they prefer to be fucked.

Negotiated rules – These are explicitly-negotiated

agreements with resulting no-go areas for extra-curricular sexual activity. This may even get into details about named exes or named venues that are off-limits. It doesn't mean that such things won't happen, just that wronged partners have justification to feel aggrieved when the other indulges in these activities. These tightly-policed arrangements might attempt to deal with areas of sexual activity where trust was previously damaged, or worries about chem-sex habits or the risk of exposure to STI.'

However, there is a darker side to the anonymity of cruising via apps, saunas and clubs and a suggestion that gay male non-monogamy is partly propagated by a commercial sex industry. Thirty-two-year-old Kevin told me, 'If Grindr had existed when I was a teen, I would've got into a lot of trouble. When all you one-hundred percent have in common is sexuality, is it a surprise that products for gay men appeal to sexual conquest? As "gay" is becoming more institutional and less political in its identity, how else can people make money off gay male insecurity than by selling sex and desire?'

He went on to say, 'Among friends my age and younger, there seems to be a trend developing towards sexual monogamy.' So perhaps, then, the popularity of open relationships and anonymous sex is waning. Maybe the bathhouses of old will become an ancient myth in a few generations' time.

Also thirty-two years old, acclaimed poet Dean Atta

recently posted on Facebook, 'Monogamy is my thing. I don't care if it's not cool, seen as old-fashioned or part of a system of oppression. My heart wants what it wants.' When we chatted further about it, he admitted that going on dates and asking 'are you monogamous?' had limited his options and forced him to write many people off. 'People think you're asking them to marry them then and there,' he laughed.

Like me, he admits to not even knowing the word 'monogamy' until he heard, a few years ago, that alternatives existed. 'A relationship is such an important part of life, why compromise? No-one's telling me monogamy is easy but perhaps it's a case of better the devil you know.'

It was his informed selection of monogamy that struck me. Maybe I, too, could find a happier way to settle upon fidelity if I was aware of my options and was in control of my own choice.

Certainly, even though my own periods of gay-man-esque promiscuity had been fun and empowering, I'd always reverted to a default of seeking an exclusive partnership. The only time I'd behaved just a little bit like Peter was in the year just before I started comedy. Twelve life-affirming and stress-busting casual flings in as many months hardly made me Tiger Woods. Yet, by lesbian standards, I felt a little slutty and all the better for it. It wasn't uncommon back then for me to fuck, pick my clothes up and leave without the niceties of conversation, cuddles and a cuppa.

Sometimes I barely knew the name of my partner, Sometimes, they commented on my bite marks or bruises left over from the previous night's action.

For once, I'd managed to shut out my own feminist outrage at objectifying my fellow women. That was the trouble with being a lesbian. You wanted to fuck women yet felt lousy and un-sisterly if you inadvertently fucked them over. It was probably no accident that it was precisely that time in my life that I felt invigorated and confident enough to launch myself into the world of stand-up. Yet that was a year when I was single. Things were easy then.

Once I met Sarah, that was it. I hardwired my brain to want only her. I was ruined for casual sex forever. Which would have been fine, had we stayed together.

I knew that to answer fully my questions about my own ability to be monogamous or not, about my identity, about the excruciating distance I felt from Jen, I would have to dig deeper. Painful as it would be, I would have to look back at the relationship that changed *everything*...

PaRT 2

HOW I *REALLY* GOT INTO THIS MESS...

THE RELATIONSHIP THAT CHANGED *EVERYTHING*

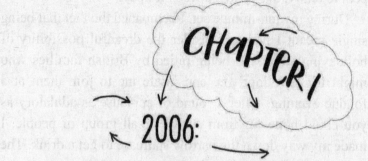

CHAPTER 1

2006:

THE HECKLER AND THE DARK-HAIRED FRIEND

The Ship of Fools, held in a tiny shabby room above The Ship pub on Borough Road, was an example of the worst type of comedy gig in London, often populated by more performers than genuine punters. Two women sat near the front, one of them amiably heckling every act.

In the first of several intervals, the heckler rushed up to me and slurred, 'You were brilliant!'

'I haven't been on yet,' I said.

Not to be deterred, she tried to engage me with an anecdote about how one of her neighbours on her Elephant and Castle estate had once tried to get her attention by firing an air rifle through her letterbox. Perhaps she was hoping to end up featuring in my material, every heckler's dream.

I wanted to escape down to the bar. Yet there was something about her dark-haired friend that was sweet, shy, cute, a little bit drunk… but intriguing. She shot me a smile that seemed to say, 'Sorry about my mate. We are nice people really. We're just a wee bit tipsy.'

During my ten-minute set, I bemoaned the fact that being single meant I had to consider the dreadful possibility of holidaying alone and being pitied by British families who might try to 'adopt' me and invite me to join them at a fondue evening. After a round of applause as adulatory as you could hope for from such a small group of people, I made my way down the narrow staircase to get a drink. The dark-haired woman chased after me.

'I'll go on holiday with you if you like.'

For someone so clearly 'the shy one' to her more exuberant blonde friend, this seemed like a ballsy gambit and took me by surprise. Listening to her speak made me focus on her thin, delicate mouth and perfect teeth. I realised that I'd been silent just a moment too long.

'Okay,' I blurted.

'I'm Sarah.'

'I'm Rosie... Well, I guess you know that already... It's not like I'm famous enough to have a stage name yet.'

She told me she was in a country band and invited me to her own gig the following evening. I was already booked but promised to look them up.

Later, I lay spread-eagled on the threadbare carpet in my tiny tumbledown flat listening to Midlake's *Van Occupanther* and dreaming of this hint of a new love interest.

For a couple of weeks I was so invested in comedy that I'd almost forgotten about Sarah. Yet I only had a month or so before I was due to head to Edinburgh Fringe for my debut solo run. I set that as my deadline to seduce her and make her my girlfriend. Edinburgh already signalled a million deadlines – getting the show slick and rehearsed, signing off my posters, sending out a press release. Why not add another challenge into the mix? After I got back, the momentum would be gone. If my peers' Fringe stories were to be believed, I would probably be suffering from flu, trench foot and liver disease by then. She might find someone else in the meantime. This was my moment to act. I grinned inwardly at my own sense of purpose, emboldened by news hot off the press that I'd made it through to the Funny Women final, to be held at The Comedy Store.

I hadn't heard anything from Sarah so thought I'd better take matters into my own hands and email her through her band's website to invite her to my gig at Moonbow Jakes, a delightful bohemian café bar in Brockley.

I often liked to add a small element of risk to the journey to a gig in order to kick-start the adrenaline I needed to find my comedy persona. In dusky light, the shortcut across Peckham Rye Common and through the estate carried just the right amount of rebellion. A group of teenage boys aimlessly kicked a football into the basketball court fencing. We were in the midst of a rare London heatwave and everyone was maximising their time spent outdoors. An older woman progressed slowly across the courtyard, her gait rendered lopsided by the heaviness of a plastic bag full of several pints of milk.

'Maybe I should offer to help her?' I thought to myself. 'Nah, I'll be late.'

I was cutting it fine time-wise, just to ramp up my cortisol. I knew my body and what it craved. I was becoming addicted to the cycle of pre-gig nerves, onstage high, followed by comedown.

As I walked across the railway bridge that ran high above the line out to the suburbs, I made a promise to myself. If Sarah turned up, I was going to kiss her. I was pretty confident that she would show, even though we had steered around any sense of the invitation being an official 'date'. The venue had a fairy-lit backyard, which would empty for last orders. That would be my opportunity. I had a plan.

John, the café owner, always seemed a little too eager when greeting female performers. 'Hello Rosie!' he smiled, his glasses rising up his face to meet his curly black fringe. 'Fancy a drink on the house?'

'Don't mind if I do... Red wine?'

As he poured me a generous tumbler of house plonk, I surveyed the room. Sarah was sitting, almost too eagerly, on the sofa at the front. My plan was on.

I sat next to her, not touching but just close enough to signal my interest.

When the evening stumbled towards eleven, I whispered,

'Come outside a minute.' John shot me a quizzical smile as he wiped glasses with a grubby tea-towel and I swaggered past the bar. Silently, Sarah followed.

I knew I didn't have long so just went for it, pressing her up against the fence in a wild embrace, the air now balmy and less sweltering. It felt so heady being able to take the initiative in a way that previous lovers had somehow never allowed. I rather liked this new, predatory me. Sarah didn't seem to be complaining either.

We must have been there for a while but it seemed like no time had passed at all when we were interrupted by a brusque matronly waitress leaning out of the window and banging a saucepan, shouting 'closing in five minutes, girls.'

We drifted our way to the bus stop holding hands. I felt a new chapter starting. For years, I'd been desperately fighting the clock trying to achieve things before I got too old. Yet for a moment, time stopped and held us in a carefree glow as opportunity unfurled in front of us like a golden magic carpet. Or perhaps it was the just the headlights of the 343.

CHAPTER 2

NO MORE FAIRYTALES

There's no doubt in my mind that, in its infancy at least, my connection with Sarah was the most conventionally 'fairytale' relationship I've had to date. Surely, though, all these dreamlike memories of magic and sunny British summer evenings are the work of an unhinged fantasist, my brain addled and high on romantic love – a state that Freud once described as a 'temporary psychosis'. There was no rational discussion of one another's life goals and guiding principles, no compatibility analysis, no thinking, just attraction and instinct.

Yet this is the person whose name I begrudgingly have to offer up when asked, 'Who is the love of your life?' Because most people who ask that question mean, 'Who is the person who made your tummy flip when you first kissed?' or 'Who is the person it felt utterly right to hold and gaze at adoringly?'

I would probably have fallen head over heels for anyone I met at that moment. I was thriving. I was in love with me, with my exciting life as an 'up-and-coming' comedian, with my new friends, with possibility. 2006 really was an untypically hot, dry summer. I felt ready to make the big commitment and be bowled over by the idea of being with someone. Even if I met the wrong person, it was the *right time*.

I didn't want to worry too much whether this was a relationship I wanted to take forward long term. I assumed that the intensity of feeling, the reassuring sense of being so present and alive, meant that I *had to*. So I did what I thought I was supposed to do and actively chose someone, hardwiring my brain to desire only her and start daydreaming about moving in together and sharing a life. There was no 'undo' button for this kind of programming. This was all or nothing. This was life or death. But I didn't really want to die before I was forty. So it'd better work out, right?

Says Qazi, 'I think that the early high you get from being in the beginnings of a relationship can drive decisions that are not optimal. And being on a high in life in general can drive us into relationships that are not optimal in the first place. Think about other rewarding behaviours, like food. You might feel that you deserve a pudding or that extra glass of wine when something goes well. The original high sweeps up all other decision-making with it.

I wonder if that high means that you don't really care how authentic your romantic relationship is... or at least you don't attend to the negative features. That could be adaptive and a trick evolution uses to make you reproduce.'

Some studies have investigated a phenomenon nicknamed 'love at first fright'. Individuals who had just got off a rollercoaster at an amusement park gave greater attractiveness ratings to photographs of strangers than those who hadn't yet been on the ride. They mistook the high of the scary, thrilling experience for feelings of desire. The unpredictable whirlwind of comedy had played a similar practical joke on me. I had been fooled into a relationship with a total stranger, without applying any sort of robust filtering process whatsoever.

Perhaps, then, a more useful question for me would be, 'Who is the best *friend* you've ever had?' This is definitely not Sarah. She's inflicted more psychological damage on me than any enemy could ever hope to. To be fair, I don't think it was intentional. These are the natural ravages of unrealistic expectations and poor communication that result from being misinformed about what a real relationship looks like.

Romantic films always seem to end just as the golden couple finally get together against all odds. As if everything is going to be fine from that moment on. Yeah right! With the exception of Richard Linklater's brilliant *Before Midnight*, barely any love stories showcase the petty domestic squabbles, squashed dreams and compromises that follow. The final part of the director's naturalistic trilogy starring Ethan Hawke and Julie Delpy, *Before Midnight* closes ambiguously with the couple, nine years into their relationship, at an outdoor restaurant in Greece. Her character Celine muses on how their (or particularly his) romantic fantasies will never be matched by the imperfection of reality. Says Alain de Botton, 'We seem to know far too much about how love starts, and recklessly little about how it might continue.'

Meanwhile, Facebook does no better at representing the genuine ups and downs of spending your life with a fellow human. My newsfeed is littered with nauseating over-sharers who I'd have a lot more patience with if they balanced every sugary anniversary post with an acknowledgment of how passion can wane when you discover that your partner has vomited in your shoe. I can't believe I'm the only person this has happened to... Anyone?

One of the people I was particularly fascinated to meet and chat to after my show in Edinburgh was writer Helen Croydon. In her book *Screw the Fairytale*, she ponders modern society's bizarre obsession with finding 'the one' and how, for some of us, a white wedding and a couple of kids really isn't the utopian ideal at all. 'I hate to sound unromantic', she says, 'but whether we choose to stay in a relationship or not is just an equation. I liked being in love very much but not enough to give up the freedom and opportunism of being single.'

She also points out how, for much of history, marriage was more concerned with the mundanities of practical and economic survival than with 'magical connection'. Passionate love affairs were kept separate. 'The idea that you could share intimacies, joys and sorrows with the same person with whom you share your home, family life, domestic chores, children and inheritance was considered unrealistic, dull or even threatening.'

Ironically, there is a synergy between these older principles and the seemingly more new and radical ideas in the poly community. Both accept that there won't be one incredible superhero who can meet our every need forever. But whereas our grandparents were either compromising and putting up with it, or having secret liaisons on the side, my poly friends would suggest openly-negotiated multiple connections as a potential antidote to the crushing disappointment of pursuing the exclusive, lifelong (quite probably non-existent) dream.

Even Kinsey realised that his 1950s studies of sex were separate from any explanation of love itself, which he thought should be left to the philosophers and poets. Love is not a reliable commodity that can be scientifically scrutinised and evaluated. Surely then it's not one that we should base all of our most important rational life decisions on?

In *Modern Romance*, Aziz Ansari adeptly demonstrates

that the shift in what we seek in a life partner can be illustrated along generational lines in couples still alive today. Everything seemed to change around fifty years ago, during the Swinging Sixties. The 'seniors' he interviewed got married young and selected a spouse because they seemed 'nice' or 'had a good job'. 'Waiting for true love was a luxury', he says, 'that many, especially women, could not afford.'

Whereas the younger generation had spent more time playing the field, weighing up options and only settled down when they truly felt that they had found their missing 'other half' – ironically an even more old-school notion, dating back to Greek mythology and Zeus splitting four-legged, two-headed humans in two. The true test will be whether these partnerships last once the delusion of hormonal overdrive has passed.

***

Back in my cold, real life in 2014, as opposed to the rose-tinted past, I felt acutely alone. Katy was long gone, in romantic terms at least. Yet I wondered if my decision to move in with Jen had been based on the high of effectively being in two 'relationships'. But what was I to do? If I had jumped ship and run off with Katy, I'd have faced all the same problems with her. There was no real solution. Neither of them replaced Sarah. But the two of them together had temporarily been a reasonable enough salve for my wounds. In combination, they had made my limbo tolerable.

I had barely spent much time in the house as I'd been so busy touring and then doing Edinburgh. So I'd deliberately taken some time off in September to unpack boxes of old CDs and books. Jen was putting in long days at the office and barely had the energy to eat and watch an hour of TV news before crashing out every evening, her exhaustion seeming like a convenient cover for her disengagement from me. Yet the charity organisation she poured herself into was such a worthy cause, it seemed almost immoral to question her work-life balance. I sought out vicarious human company in the walled garden in Brockwell Park, reading, writing, people-watching and soaking up the last days of summer.

I held a spontaneous birthday party and, although some of my best friends made it, I felt more aware of the absences, the holes in my heart... Sarah, Katy, Anna.

I, for one, had been well and truly burned by going along with the modern trend to search for perfection and passion. I had been conned. My boom-and-bust serial monogamy cycle had turned more into a spiral, downwards into despair at the pointlessness and wastefulness of it all. I thought the oldies had it right. Companionate marriage sounded like a solid idea, built on the firmer foundations of trust and friendship than the sheer, temporary lunacy of love. If everyone else 'made do' and compromised on romance, then perhaps I could too.

Yet it was impossible to declare this openly and honestly

as a strategy in my relationship with Jen. A non-romantic primary partnership was something to be vilified or, worse, pitied. 'You have to break up,' said friends, shaking their heads. Spam emails from dating sites flooded my inbox screaming, 'Are you with your sexual soulmate?' 'No,' I thought, 'and thank God, too, because the closest I got to a sexual soulmate was Sarah... and she turned out to be an arse.' A particularly crude missive stated, 'Your vagina doesn't lie!' I was not sure that either this email, or my vagina, had my best interests at heart.

Yet idiotic as these not-so-subliminal messages were, they fuelled my grief for romance, and consequently for Sarah, enough to make it untenable. Thus my memories of her became heightened, an unwanted movie playing over and over in my head. She had become a fictional character, a muse.

I was at war with love. I felt let down by it as a concept, my rational, pragmatic relationship with Jen a direct reaction to the irrational one I'd had with Sarah. I wanted to reason with romance and sent emails to my old defunct address, out there into the ether.

'Dear Love, Why are you like this?'

But perhaps the fact that I was using my own former email meant that what I was really saying was:

'Dear Me, Why did you do this to yourself?'

The narrator in the wonderful documentary *Notes On Blindness* asks himself, 'Was I going to live in reality or live in nostalgia?' as he wrestles to accept his physical situation. That line in particular made me sob.

It struck me that love, when it's as obsessive as my posthumous desire for Sarah was, really is a type of blindness. I was living in nostalgia. I was so seduced by what might have been that I couldn't see what could still be. What could be with Jen.

I designed another road sign for the comedy show: a cartoon fairy, replete with a little floaty dress and magic wand... and a bloody great red line through her.

CHAPTER 3
BATGIRL IN EDINBURGH

It felt like I was going to be gone for an eternity. Yet if Sarah and I were officially 'in love' then we would have to write, phone and she would visit. I willed it to happen and enjoyed this sense of being in the driver's seat. We were hurtling along the romantic highway at breakneck speed with careless abandon. 'Rush, rush, rush... Push, push, push... Make her fall for you,' was my mantra. I had no idea what my plan was after that initial goal had been achieved.

The surge of positive energy I got from performing fuelled the connection. I had always found it impossible to fall in love from a standing start, with nothing else going on in my life. Yet now I was really on the move, racing towards the future. The unreality of rising up the comedy ranks allowed me access to a dream world of opportunity and free boozy parties and energised me enough to take Sarah with me. It didn't occur to me that setting myself up as a superhero might backfire when things started to go wrong or when normality set back in. For now, the stars were aligned. I was invincible.

Finally, the middle weekend of the Festival came around, marked with a tiny, inked love heart in my diary, and I was running to Waverley station. I managed to position myself on the platform at exactly the door she alighted from. We stood awkwardly before greeting, as if we didn't know each other. We didn't, I suppose.

After my show, we went to see Richard Hawley at old converted church, The Liquid Room, on steeply sloping Victoria Street. We adored his album *Coles Corner* and often changed the words of 'Born Under a Bad Sign' to 'bat' sign. We seemed to have developed a series of in-jokes about the nocturnal flying mammals and she had given herself the unlikely superhero nickname of Batgirl.

Back in London, we christened a building near City Hall 'the bat tower' as we could both see it from our bedroom windows. It had a rooftop barometer: a beacon that changed colour with the air pressure... or with the power of our love, as we preferred to think. Our imaginary colony of bat friends resided there and flew back and forth with love messages.

The earthiness of someone who enjoyed nature appealed to me, even if it was a little nerdy. It kept me grounded in the competitive and paranoid world of performance. Our private joy shielded me. It didn't matter so desperately much what people thought of my show – and when it didn't matter so desperately much, people liked it more. The dopamine high of romantic love allowed me the sense of childlike wonder at the world that you need in order to write comedy.

But... as with all great love stories, there was a ruddy, great obstacle in our path.

'I tried to tell her about me and Julie when I was nineteen. But she just said I should never mention it ever again. So I haven't.'

Sarah was perched on the edge of my comically tiny, uncomfortable sofa. It barely seated two people, particularly as it had started to sag in the middle. For the first time, a deep and fragile sorrow was visible within my girlfriend, behind the excitable sheen of new love. She seemed to adore her family. Yet they didn't want to know who she really was. Or, at least, her mum had decided that her dad definitely wouldn't want to. And that she would do her level best to ignore and forget all about her only daughter trying to come out.

'Oh God, poor you,' I whispered, squeezing in next to her.

My heart sank, not just for her but for me too. It was as if a dark, gloomy cloud had discreetly floated into my glorious, technicolour new life that I'd done so well at inventing. This secrecy was a real threat to my own happiness. I knew that instinctively. I'd always been so lucky with my own family's acceptance. Yet I'd come across plenty of women whose parents' homophobia had devastated and ultimately destroyed most of their sexual relationships. Blood was often thicker than water... even intolerant blood.

My Gaydar Girls dating profile clearly stated that I was seeking 'someone who's out to their family'. It was a deal-breaker. I didn't want to sneak around, arrested in a furtive asexual adolescence. I was an adult with a sex life. Get over it, world. Sarah hadn't seen my list of requirements, of course. She was a real-life meeting. Hence we hadn't had this discussion until I was too emotionally committed to retreat.

As I sighed and cuddled her, an incoming text pinged on my phone. My friend Rachel was having a civil partnership.

'Really happy for you!' I replied.

It seemed an exquisitely agonising, heart-wrenching paradox that just as wider society was taking huge steps forward in lesbian and gay equality, homophobia had well and truly landed in my personal world. Still... if anyone was going to face adversity head-on in wilful defiance, it was me. I started to feel confident that Sarah's parents would see how happy her new 'friendship' with me was making her. Surely they would gradually welcome me in and understand its true nature. Even though we'd known each other a matter of months, we were convinced that we were soulmates. We wrote love letters. We adored one another. They couldn't question all that. It was real.

But as Christmas, and then the Easter holiday, passed and I waved her off each time on the train to Wales alone, I realised that no headway was being made.

She tried to reassure me by telling me that her parents had enjoyed the film *Brokeback Mountain*. I thought this was hardly giving a positive sense of how well gay relationships could turn out.

I just couldn't fully fit into her life. I imagined looking at childhood photos of her, her old bedroom: the normal things that give you that extra context, that extra dimension of knowing and loving someone. I felt invisible, powerless. I could only delight in the smallest of victories when I heard second-hand about the awkward dinner conversation I'd prompted by booking a holiday in Lesvos.

I did the only thing I knew how and focused on work. If I could earn and achieve enough, maybe I could buy her family's approval. Never mind comedy, this would be the biggest challenge of all.

CHAPTER 4

WHAT MAKES US GAY?

As the next two years passed, the concealment of the relationship chipped away at our happiness, my sense of self and confidence dismantled by the lack of control that the situation afforded me. Secrecy had catalysed our love's exponential decay. I confided in fellow performer Jen Brister when she gave me a lift home one night from Ed comedy, a lovely little gig in Forest Hill. 'This is no good, Rosie,' she said. 'It's going to break up the relationship.'

As a goodwill concession, Sarah emailed me with the family phone number. But I felt pretty clear that she had only sent it because she trusted me *never* to dial it.

We talked about moving in together to overcome our inertia and force some sense of legitimacy. We viewed part-buy flats in Peckham and Brockley. Yet I couldn't face the falsehood of being presented as a 'friend' or a 'flatmate' and issued an ultimatum that we couldn't proceed until she came out. I felt like I was waiting for permission to live my adult life. Thoughts of buying property also prompted discussions about finances, highlighting yet another area in which we were disallowed as a viable couple. We were hardly well off.

The holiday in Lesvos had its beautiful moments. Yet when she accidentally deleted all her photos of the trip, it seemed to reinforce our utter invisibility. I lay awake at night staring up at the hotel ceiling, the first time I was really made aware that we were no longer having sex.

The transience of being away seemed to emphasise the flimsiness of what we had together. I drifted into a restless dream. Our small hotel was transformed into a sprawling luxury complex. I peered down from a balcony into a glistening swimming pool several floors below. 'Ah no,' I gasped as the room key fell from my hand, down and down into the pool. Morphing into the cartoon physique of a Lara Croft action figure, I dived in. Yet as I elegantly splashed into the water, weeds grew and caught around my feet. I could see the key but I couldn't reach it. Gasping for breath, I pulled myself back into consciousness. It was pretty clear what the elusive key represented... happiness, sex, and a real, authentic relationship. All things that I no longer had any way of accessing.

My physical stage presence shrank accordingly. In videos and photos that were posted and shared online, I noticed that my shoulders became more hunched, almost apologetically, instead of being pushed back, open and stretching me tall. This was exactly the time when I should have been making waves, marching on in my career. Agents and producers were checking me out in the wake of competition final spots and good reviews. But they weren't seeing the real me.

As more and more time fell through my fingers, the notion of leaving Sarah receded in my mind. Now I was in so deep, I would look like an idiot for staying locked in a situation that made me miserable. So I simply *had* to turn things around and fix it.

My solution was to look to my creativity for answers. I started developing The Science Of Sex, scouring the shelves at Dulwich Library for anything on the neuroscience and psychology of attraction. I had big plans for it to double up as my breakthrough show and the magical source of answers about how to heal my connection with Sarah.

It was this frenzied research period that drew me to someone who would become a key influence in my more science-based writing and performance, Dr Qazi Rahman. His primary area of research at the time was sexual orientation.

I first spotted him in a 2008 BBC documentary which followed John Barrowman on a quest to answer the question 'What made me gay?'. With the aid of scientists, he whizzed through all kinds of theories about finger-length ratios, hair whorls and having older brothers. My curiosity was especially piqued when Qazi appeared onscreen and

Barrowman underwent some tests with him in skills such as map reading, memory, word fluency and three-dimensional shape rotation. I immediately googled him and sent an email. To my surprise, he was more than happy to make time for me to go and record an interview with him for my radio show and for me to take part in the same study that Barrowman had done.

Regarding the basis for the tests, he said:

'One of the biological theories about sexual orientation predicts that gay men should have a psychology (which includes things like cognitive abilities, personality, aptitudes, gender expression and so on) that is similar, on average, to heterosexual women. This is because they share the same direction of sexual preference (both are attracted to men). Lesbians should have a psychology that is similar to heterosexual men. So the prediction is that the cognitive abilities of gay men should be more like those of women and the cognitive abilities of lesbian women more like heterosexual men. Study after study has shown this to be case for gay men and, in certain areas of cognition and brain patterns, for lesbians (but not as strong as the findings for gay men).'

My own performance was mixed. I was poor at the mental rotation that straight men are typically good at, but somewhere in between straight men and straight women for many other tasks. I was particularly shoddy at map reading, crumbling under the pressure of the stopwatch. When it came to nightmare navigation I was out there on a limb, way beyond even the straight women and gay men. I simply can't do it without turning the damn thing round the way I'm facing! (However now that my iPhone can do this part for me, surely I win?)

As if to rub salt in the wound, Qazi printed out a graph of the results for gay men, straight men, lesbians and straight women with mine in a separate column marked 'Rosie'. As if I'm my own sexual category. Maybe he knew something I didn't.

He explained that these differences in problem-solving abilities point to differences in underlying brain structure and that sex hormones in the womb environment, and the way we respond to them, play a big role in shaping these patterns rather than just genes per se. So although there's no 'gay gene' as such, there is a strong biological suggestion that we could be born homosexual.

But before we start shouting about stereotypes, it's apparently not just a simple case of 'female-like' or 'male-like' brains: 'It's more a mosaic of gendered traits – a "gender-bending" brain if you will. And more importantly – what's wrong with male femininity and female masculinity?'

There's nothing wrong with a bit of gender-bending. However, I was really struggling to find my own place on the gender-identity spectrum, under self-induced pressure to be more androgynous than I actually was. I desperately wanted to fit in and find a sense of family and belonging within the queer community. I did my level best to push myself to the centre of the gay world, even as I saw it fragmenting. Yet somehow I didn't feel like I was the same as other lesbians.

Years earlier, a female friend called Ben had described my then-partner Alice as a 'butch-y femme' and me as a 'femme-y butch'. While I liked the neat idea of mirroring each other and it felt like a modern twist on the old-fashioned butch-femme lesbian binary, I wasn't sure this fitted me at all.

Yes, my exterior was all lipstick and mascara. But I was beginning to realise that my interior alpha drives for sex, work and creativity, the ones that Ben had seen as more masculine, actually came out of a very female energy too. I wasn't a high-femme like raven-haired poet Sophia Blackwell, a younger woman I'd once had a near-crush on. She was never to be seen in anything other than a vintage frock and heels. Even though I was more often dressed in lesbian 'uniform' of jeans and checked shirt, I celebrated being a girl and being *with* a girl.

But gay femme visibility is a tricky thing. If you don't 'look' gay, you are assumed not to be. In the 1990s, bouncers at gay clubs had often asked me, 'Do you know what kind of place this is?'

I thought I'd done the hard work by coming out and finding a female partner who was also gay. But that's only

200

the beginning. You need to find the *right* woman. And not only that, you need to find the woman that you want to *be*.

CHAPTER 5

2009:

LOVE TURNED UPSIDE DOWN

Sarah was at the bar. I smiled at revellers, absorbed the heavy bass thud of competing sound systems carried like insects on the breeze, and soaked up the last glow of fuzzy Australian evening light.

We were at Mardi Gras at the height of an adventure. Both of us were wearing straw cowboy hats donated by our hosts, something we would feel idiotic wearing back in England, yet which felt fine here. I felt in a state of utter peace, despite being surrounded by neon chaos. My gig had gone really well and I could relax.

I'll never understand what happened in those few moments that irrevocably changed the dynamic of our relationship. When you think about what creates love – a spark, a jolt of electricity, a deep recognition, a feeling that 'I know this, I've been here', an instant connection – maybe it makes sense that it can be ignited, rekindled or extinguished so quickly.

Love makes a mockery of time. It can be nurtured and sculpted over decades like a fine artist chipping away at a great work, or it can be so utterly fleeting and transient. It can leave you like a passenger on the platform running vainly alongside the departing train and forced to give in and wait for the next one, the next chance. We had flown to the other side of the world and had, metaphorically speaking, turned our hearts upside down.

Entering our third year, I was starting to feel a little trapped, a little weighed down by someone who kept spoiling my romantic fantasy by not stepping up to the plate, by not wanting to be amazing, brave and open together, by not having the vision or courage to move forward into our life.

'Come on! We can do this!' I'd say.

Yet as she turned back towards me *that* night bearing golden drinks, I felt the air escape from my atmosphere as if I no longer needed oxygen but just to breathe her. I felt my eyes become huge cinema screens zooming into close-up, her face and smile flooding my retinas like a river bursting its banks. I felt deconstructed and reconstructed, my limbs and organs rearranged in unfamiliar patterns, yet finally all in the right place. We had not consumed any drugs or much alcohol. I can only attribute this earth-shattering, heart-breaking, bewildering, time-stopping feeling to pure unadulterated love. Who needs drugs when you have this?

I say heart-breaking because intrinsically I knew that this must be the first time I had seen my girlfriend truly, deeply happy. Away from the pressures of family and work, surrounded by long-lost friends in celebratory mode, here was the woman I'd been searching for. Here was her soul. And inevitably, here also was mine. Yet this was a holiday. How could I save this, keep this, return here, mark it, bottle it?

How many times had I said 'I love you' to her before this moment? How could I say it differently now, add deeper resonance, reflect this new dimension, this extra universe of feeling that had snuck up and bolted itself onto my old version of love like a docking spaceship.

Did she even feel it too? She must have, as she looked me square in the eyes right then and made a promise. 'I'll tell them Rosie… I'll tell them about us.'

CHAPTER 6
THE TROUBLE WITH PROMISES

The trouble with promises is that they weigh heavy if you don't know how you're going to keep them.

Still hazy with jetlag, I made my way to my first gig back in London at a new-material night at The Castle pub opposite Farringdon Station. Sarah and I were in the habit of texting each other goodnight, or having a quick check-in chat, on evenings when we couldn't see each other. After my set, I raced across the road for the train home, gleefully messaging her. The new show was gearing up for its first previews and I felt excited and hopeful.

I flicked through *Time Out* on the platform, awaiting her reply. When I got myself home and still hadn't heard anything, I started to fret. 'Where was she? Who was she with?' I had entrusted my entire wellbeing to her, and she was pretty careless with it.

Eventually, my phone beeped.

'I've been out with work... On my way home... Night night.'

'Can I give you a quick call?' I replied.

Without waiting for the permission I'd requested, I rang anyway. My call was declined.

This wasn't right. Since Australia, we'd been speaking daily. I needed my fix.

I tried again. Declined again.

'Talk to you tomorrow.'

I rang again.

She picked up, pissed off now.

'I'm still out. I'll speak to you tomorrow.'

'So why did you say you were on your way home?'

'Because I knew you'd be like this.'

She was right. We pushed all the wrong buttons in one another. A bit of easy-going texting could spiral within seconds into a full-blown argument, her avoidant, distant behaviour making me feel anxious, paranoid and clingy. I'd been reading about the psychology of these classic incompatible love styles. But even this understanding of the dynamic didn't equip me to alter it.

In the same way that mobile technology had facilitated our initial flirting, it now exacerbated our conflict. Its immediate, reactive nature poured kerosene on the flaming touchpaper of a row.

'For fuck's sake,' I gasped, resigned to anger rather than trying to articulate my feelings. Anyway, whenever I told her, 'don't do X because it hurts me when you do X', it seemed to make her do X even more frequently. As Alice summed it up, every time I cried on her shoulder, 'it's like Sarah's always pissing on your fire.' It was her passive-aggressive way of trying to push me away once and for all, her escape hatch from having to deliver on that reckless promise she'd made... her promise to come out.

Sarah hung up.

I stormed to bed, stewing over the question, 'why did she lie?' It wasn't an easy one to put away to the back of my mind.

A couple of weeks later on a Saturday night, the first official Science Of Sex preview was booked in for Cambridge Comedy Festival. I loved gigging in Cambridge. The bohemian audiences seemed to like my Radio 4-esque whimsy and it was always nice and easy to get home again afterwards. The gig was already a sell-out, my first for a show completely in my own name. Yet, as I sauntered across town, I felt a rising panic, my chest closing in and restricting my breathing. This wasn't pre-gig nerves. I knew and loved those. This was a greater alien grief. Sarah had gone silent again, never a good thing. I checked and checked my phone, again and again, more and more compulsively. I envisaged a huge clock in the dusky sky above me, counting down time on the relationship. I was awaiting execution. And I knew it.

Perversely, my heightened state added something to my performance. I wished I could stop time and stay under the safety of the stage lights forever, comforted by the adoring embrace of applause. All too soon, though, the show was over. I was on my way back to London and forced to return to my feelings of rejection, abandonment and worthlessness.

It was the next morning before a text arrived from Sarah. We made a tentative plan to meet later that evening. I felt temporarily appeased. But when she eventually called to postpone, my patience withered. I found myself uttering the hideous question she'd been pushing and pushing at, daring me to ask.

'You don't want to break up, do you?'

'Yeah, maybe I do.'

CHAPTER 7
NEGATIVE LOVE EQUITY AND RELATIONSHIP ANARCHY

We kept stumbling on and on. She would leave. I would woo her back with love letters and songs, driven by a huge sense of purpose. She would leave again. We were an endlessly repeating fractal pattern derived from our own set of chaotic emotional equations. Yet, unlike snowflakes, peacock feathers and nautilus shells, our output was ugly.

All the books I was reading implied that relationship happiness was based on simple exchange theory. If you subtracted the number of times you argued from the number of times you had sex and were still in credit, then you were probably doing alright. I was certain I was in a sort of negative equity. Any real, tangible value that the relationship had once held was leaking away, yet I held on to it fiercely despite its escalating cost. The logical thing to do would be to get out. If I could take control and walk away, maybe I'd be happier in the long run.

Yet one author triggered a fear in me so great that it quashed any such bold notions. Would it be *even worse* to be alone than to feel alone? American writer Lori Gottlieb certainly seemed to think so, in her article for *The Atlantic* entitled 'The case for settling for Mr Good Enough'. Although it was written primarily for a heteronormative female reader who wanted to have a family, I assumed that the principle translated for gay women. I could hardly believe what I was reading.

'Don't nix a guy based on his annoying habit of yelling "Bravo" in movie theatres. Overlook his halitosis or abysmal sense of aesthetics.'

'By forty, if you get a cold shiver down your spine at the thought of embracing a certain guy, but you enjoy his company more than anyone else's, is that settling or making an adult compromise?'

Whoa! I was nearly forty. By Gottlieb's depressing logic, I was way past the life stage at which I could afford to be picky. Maybe I just needed to 'woman up' and accept that Sarah's parents didn't want to know me. She had been so sweet, charming and kind in the beginning. Maybe if I backed down about the coming out thing, she was my 'Ms Good Enough'.

Yet at what stage did 'settling' tip into bending so far backwards that you're contorted, a completely different shape and form from the person you once were? I just didn't recognise myself any more.

***

I was lying awake in bed again, aware that my T-shirt was drenched with sweat, catapulted back into my real life and consciousness. My serially monogamous existence had been episodic and fractured. I felt buffeted around in my own narrative. I sometimes didn't even know where I was and what year it was. I looked to my right. Jen was there in the bed, sleeping soundly. I felt a temporary relief. I felt just as lost as I had in 2009. But in 2014 I had the reassuring comfort of a quest, a much bigger one than The Science of Sex had been.

I reached for my iPad to browse Facebook, trying not to wake Jen. An invite appeared in my feed to a 'Relationship Anarchy' meeting in east London. Of course it was in east London. Everything cool and alternative happened there.

It was first time I had come across the term, often abbreviated to RA, and, on the surface, it seemed very similar to polyamory. Yet it cleared up that pesky ambiguity as to whether deep platonic friendships counted. A typical relationship anarchist would simply make no distinction between their different types of multiple connections. Normative categories such as 'just friends' or 'in a relationship' were gleefully dispensed with. All emotional intimacies had value. This ideology was something that, thus far, I had been calling 'a new currency of commitment'.

Ironically, the meeting that Sunday afternoon was one of

the least anarchic I had ever been to. A mixed group of twenty-five or so people, mostly around their twenties and thirties, waited outside in an orderly queue to gain access to the building, then followed an agenda and broke into groups for further discussion. It was then that I got chatting to writer and therapist Meg-John Barker about the concept of a 'relationship escalator'.

Meg-John described how society seems to have shackled itself to the normative idea that any relationship worth its salt continually progresses through a series of recognised stages – from courtship, to declarations of love and defining as a 'couple' to moving in together, marriage and kids. The escalator only moves in one direction, often rather quickly, with no recognised valid option to pause or step back. Unless you keep moving forwards and upwards together, you need to break up and start again with a new partner.

This hit home. It was exactly this kind of exhausting, high-pressure, high-stakes slippery snakes-and-ladders game that had perpetuated my own lifelong serial monogamy. Meg-John and other activists were keen to present alternatives to what felt like a very enforced structure. How many times do we say, 'Where is this relationship *going*?'

Jen and I were not going anywhere. But maybe that was okay. Staying still felt safe for now. And maybe one day, if we needed to, we'd be able to cruise backwards safely together towards a cushioned, collaborative landing, rather than being rudely catapulted off the escalator like unwanted, failed travellers. Or worse still, we'd end up emotionally jousting and ultimately pushing each other off.

The meeting wasn't *all* an idyllic utopia of empathy and agreement. I read out a section of my *New Statesman* article entitled 'Isn't it Time we Admitted We're All a Bit Poly?' which I'd just written and felt rather proud of. In a matter of hours, it had accumulated thousands of likes, shares and comments.

'What if we viewed our relationships as a pyramid structure with our primary partner at the top and a host of lovers, spiritual soulmates, colleagues and acquaintances beneath that?' I said.

'Great piece... but why a pyramid?' one of the group asked.

I hadn't prepared myself for being challenged on this. In my warm excitable glow of newly discovering all things poly, I assumed that everyone interrogating monogamy and holding it to account was on the same page.

I had inadvertently revealed myself to be clinging on to the capitalist structures of hierarchy. I wanted to see Jen as my primary because it made practical and economic sense to live together and share resources. I remembered asking my comedian friend Zoe Lyons about monogamy and she'd said instantly, 'It's just splitting the bills, isn't it?'

I also worried whether Jen would want to be with me if she didn't feel that she was my number one... or I with her,

215

if I wasn't hers in some way. Dave Pickering told me how one of his lovers once said, 'I don't want to be a second fiddle.' 'But,' said Dave, 'everyone is a different instrument.' Still, if even a group of right-on relationship anarchists couldn't play in complete harmony, I wasn't sure that humans were unselfish enough to comply with this analogy.

I wanted desperately to throw away the relationship rulebook... but only if I could rip out and stash a few of my favourite pages under my pillow. To keep forging forwards with my commitment to viewing and doing relationships differently, I would have to remind myself how heartbreaking life on the normative escalator had been, injured and bleeding onto the slowly morphing, disappearing steps, wounded by Sarah's broken promise.

CHAPTER 8

WINTER

As winter descended with full force, Sarah took pity on me staying in my poorly insulated icebox of a flat. On the bus, she pressed a set of keys into my hand and beamed at me, 'Stay. At least until the weather improves.'

I spent that December working on a new show in Borough's John Harvard Library and looking forward to Sarah coming home from work each day. There was just the hint of a rekindling.

We watched out the window as silent gentle snowflakes crept along the lawn then went out to make fresh footprints, relishing the creaking sound of those first steps. We were laughing again, connecting, holding hands.

Yet our worst time of year beckoned – Christmas. I felt a huge pang for the seasonal magic I'd felt as a child, enraptured by tiny multicoloured glass trumpets hanging on my grandma's tree. If you blew into them, they actually made a musical sound. Now I had to spend Christmas alone with Dad, unable to have contact with my partner.

Out of the blue, Sarah promised that she would make the big announcement about us over her family's Boxing Day meal. Wow! Maybe everything was going to work out. I would have my heroic fairytale ending after all.

I waited with baited breath, clutching my mobile phone, only to get a text late in the evening saying, 'Sorry, I couldn't go through with it... It's a time for family.'

'But you *are* my family,' I replied.

I could almost see her physically recoiling at the burden this statement would place on her. Back in London, I started to make plans for New Year's Eve.

The cold spell subsided so I moved back into my flat and Sarah agreed to come to me to see the year in. We watched the midnight fireworks together from my window with a hot toddy, occasionally glancing over to our bat tower and smiling.

We spent a blissfully peaceful few days together, cushioned away from the outside world, eating, reading newspapers and watching films. 'You mean everything to me,' she said one evening as we squashed up together on my hopeless sofa. Everything felt back on course. I had righted the ship.

But less than twenty-four hours after she'd kissed me goodbye, an email wormed its way into my universe like a

218

terrible virus and shattered my sense of calm. The subject line read 'pushing and pulling'. I already knew it wasn't going to be good.

Words danced about the screen in a seasick sense of unreality.

'I have been distant and trying to push you into getting rid of me.'

'I think we should recognise the end of our relationship as hard as that is now.'

This *couldn't* happen. This undid everything I believed in and was fighting for, everything that had defined my sense of purpose. This invalidated *me*.

But even I knew there was a real sense of finality this time. I picked up her toothbrush and carefully and deliberately dropped it into the bin. She was gone.

And now I was nothing.

CHAPTER 9

BUT *I* LOOSENED THE LID

A few years later, deep into the ambiguous emotional rabbit hole of my relationship with Jen, I was in the pub having lunch with my friend Rachel. Considering that she was a teetotal friend, we seemed to meet there rather a lot. But it was often on an occasion when I was in shock and needed a drink. I was bemoaning the fact that I'd heard on the gossipy lesbian grapevine that Sarah's parents were starting to accept her sexuality.

In fact, several of my exes had eventually overcome the hurdles that made them dysfunctional partners. But only once they had broken up with me and it was too late for me to benefit from the change. Each of them went on to be a better, nicer girlfriend for the next person they went out with. How annoying.

Alice curbed her drinking after years of me challenging her about it. While another eccentric musician ex conquered the agoraphobia which had severely restricted both our professional touring activities and social life.

'It's a bit like when you're trying to open a jar,' giggled Rachel, trying to help me to see the funny side. 'And you hand it to someone else and go "Can you open this?" and they say "Oh, it's really easy!" and it's really infuriating because you loosened the lid.'

'Yes, that's exactly it!' I said. 'I did loosen all those lids!'

Yet, behind the laughter, what I actually *felt* like was a jar smashed into a million pieces.

Over four years on, I was still reeling from the brutal and one-sided nature of Sarah's execution of our relationship. Pondering a potential alternative, I started a Facebook discussion thread and mooted the idea of a 'decompression year'. Surely a consensually-agreed twelve-month untangling could be fairer than plunging one party so suddenly into grief? A relationship should be a collaborative effort. Except in cases of physical violence and abuse, where fleeing becomes essential for survival, shouldn't the conversation about an ending be two-way?

The suggestion met with puzzlement from many monogamous friends about how on earth such rules could be negotiated. But then I chatted to comedian friend Charlie Duncan Saffrey at his Stand-up Philosophy night. While he's not strictly a fan of the word 'polyamory', he has written intelligently about the 'many kinds of love, which can overlap in ways that needn't be exclusive or finite'. Perhaps our 'post-romantic' winding-down phase could be one of these types of love and needs to be given the respect and space of something like a decompression year. He knew a straight couple who had employed that sort of idea. The woman in this case had given her boyfriend several months to acclimatise to the separation, while still spending time with him, talking and hanging out. It had helped him, and ultimately them both.

New York psychotherapist Esther Perel has recently called for greater 'relationship accountability' in the wake of new trends such as 'ghosting' and 'icing', which respectively see partners disappearing without explanation or finding excuses to suspend a relationship and put it on hold.

An even more recent term to be added to the lexicon of bad behaviour is 'breadcrumbing'. This describes a person leading you on with flattering and flirty texts, calls and plans to meet up... but they never act on any of it. Author and relationship expert Susan Winter says, 'Breadcrumbing is the conscious act of leading someone on for the thrill of the ego boost. It's the hot cycle in the game of hot and cold.'

Meanwhile, Aziz Ansari found that seventy-three percent of a group of young adults, the majority of whom had already confessed to dumping people by text and social media, admitted that they would be upset if someone broke up with them that way. Maybe it's that simple. Treat people as you would like to be treated.

If we extend a sense of responsibility to online dating and short-term flings, maybe we should build a more compassionate community where we offer a suitable substitute match to everyone we reject. We could offset our romantic footprint, if you like. It's not a million miles from a popular comedy-industry ethos whereby you offer a replacement of an equivalent quality and experience level whenever you drop out of a gig at the last minute.

The big new player in our language around breakups, of course, is the term 'conscious uncoupling'. It was devised by author and family therapist Katherine Woodward Thomas as a way to have 'an honourable or respectful' separation with 'minimal harm to all involved'. The phrase made headlines in 2014 when Gwyneth Paltrow and Chris Martin used it to describe their separation. At the time, I was among the bemused detractors. Was it just a hippy-dippy euphemism? Wasn't a breakup bound to be easier if you had money and several houses?

Yet it's hard to deny it's worked well for them. 'We're still very much a family, even though we don't have a romantic relationship. He's like my brother,' she told *Glamour* magazine. They've holidayed together and been photographed smiling and laughing like dear old friends. Perhaps surprisingly, it hasn't prevented either from moving on to new partners.

A male comedian friend explained to me how his thinking around separations had changed over recent years. Previously he'd gone along with the idea that 'if you split up you must scream and shout and never talk to the other person again'. Yet he and his wife had admitted that 'this might all be over but we would still want to be friends – because at heart, we are'.

If Jen and I were going to move on, maybe some form of conscious uncoupling could be a way forward for us too. After all, I thought of her as 'family'. I wanted to find some way to protect that without excluding us from all future possibility of romantic love or sex. Until now, polyamory had presented itself as the only answer... but, now here was a loosely more 'monogamous' solution.

We sat on the sofa one Sunday evening in jeans and scuzzy weekend jumpers, me cradling her legs over mine and gently stroking them. 'I don't think we should have sex any more,' I said.

'Oh... OK,' she seemed slightly stunned.

We were getting on so well now that we didn't bother with any sexual intimacy at all. But it still seemed important to say out loud that it just wasn't part of 'us' any more.

'I still love you. In fact, I love you more. I'm here for you. Always.'

Serial monogamy, as I'd known it, had certainly been an unhappy, exhausting lifestyle. I would never have chosen it. So I wanted to do everything in my power to avoid yet another conventional ending. I loved Jen and wanted a lifelong connection, just with altered parameters.

It's not like we can erase our past loves, like Kate Winslet and Jim Carrey attempt to do in the film *Eternal Sunshine of the Spotless Mind*. And why would we want to? Those memories are a part of us. They form our history, and therefore, form us. So I was concerned to read neuro-ethicist Brian D. Earp writing in *New Scientist* that there *could* be cases where there's a moral argument for 'anti-love' biotechnology – in other words, a pill to help us forget an ex. This isn't science fiction but a genuine debate. In 2014, he said, 'there are lots of ways to get over someone... But if other ways have failed, and anti-love drugs could help to alleviate suffering and prepare a person to move on with life, there could be good reasons for using them.'

Because I'd grown up with parents who stayed together, separations just weren't on my radar or in my DNA. That's why they felt so alien and wrong to me. But I think I'd still rather feel the pain and grapple to understand it. When I'm visiting Dad and setting the table, I still occasionally happen upon an old Valentine's card from Mum to him tucked away in a drawer among old Christmas napkins and bedraggled Easter chicks. A double dagger to the heart – partly because she's no longer here and that spidery handwriting is all we have left... then also because I know *I've* never been loved like that.

Meanwhile Jen, just a few years younger than me, hit the

divorce epidemic. 'All my friends at school had parents who were separated,' she says. So, for an altogether different reason, she too was keen to avoid an archetypal ill-tempered severing. She had seen it at close quarters.

The huge downside of serial monogamy is serial breakup. What's more, we are reinforcing the idea in other couples' minds every time we separate. A talk by Susan David, author of *Emotional Agility*, introduced me to the idea of a social contagion effect. If we get divorced, then our friends are more likely to. Not only that, we are also more likely to end our subsequent relationships. Divorce rates increase exponentially, once you isolate figures for second and third marriages. As American comedian Mike Birbiglia points out, '*That's* a learning curve.' We really do realise how bat-shit-crazy this long-term love business is. But isn't that exactly why we should stick out our first marriages rather than chase our tails in ever-decreasing circles?

At what point do we have a responsibility to stay together, not just for the sake of the kids, our partner or ourselves, but for the good of our social community? A group of long-term gay male friends I know spent years holidaying together, partying, supporting one another, hanging out and having meals together. Yet when a central couple separated and found new partners, this network of companionship was disbanded. Despite everyone's best efforts to remain amicable and not 'take sides', the impact was suffered keenly by the whole group. The breakup had eroded an entire landscape of friendship.

If, ultimately, we are going to be just as dissatisfied with *any* partner once the initial few months of frenzied passion are over, then what is the point of breaking up and moving on? In other words, what is the point of serial monogamy? Unless we are going to be conscious and compassionate enough to continue close ties with ex-partners, I can't see one.

To interrogate how I saw Jen and me being 'family' in the future, I needed to evaluate what that concept meant to me. I felt prompted to delve even further back into my romantic history and look at my relationship with Alice, the partner who was an integral part of my first attempt to create my own alternative family setup, in the form of an indie band. Yep, long before I turned to comedy, I was the archetypal wistful lesbian with an acoustic guitar. Come with me in a time machine, if you will, back to my Britpop years.

paRt 3

HOW I GOT INTO THE MESS
THAT GOT ME INTO A MESS

...THE FIRST *BIG* RELATIONSHIP

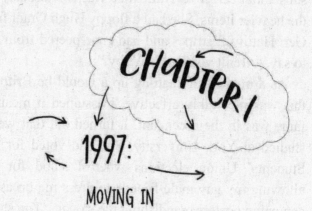

CHAPTER 1

1997:

MOVING IN

The Verve's 'Bitter Sweet Symphony' pounded through our ceiling for the fifth time that day. Our new neighbour seemed friendly enough though. He poked his head cheekily around our propped-open door, squinting as if unfamiliar with being conscious and upright in daylight hours.

'Hi, I'm Chris from upstairs. Give me a knock later if you wanna share some beers and weed.'

'Marvellous,' beamed Alice, her voice sounding extra posh against his Mancunian rasp.

We could hardly complain about his noise as we dragged my vintage amp, several guitars, keyboards and my extensive CD collection downstairs to the basement flat... along with, bizarrely, a life-size cardboard cut-out of Texas singer Sharleen Spiteri. We threw her out in the recycling a while later, an action which coincidentally heralded her substantial career revival. Alice was chivalrously taking all the heavier items. She had a floppy Hugh Grant fringe with Geri Halliwell stripes and had once peered from beneath it to say, 'Aren't you Rosie Wilby?'

As a method of chatting up a would-be Britpop starlet, this was incredibly effective. I assumed it meant that my fame was in the ascendant. It turned out that we had both studied at York University. She had voted for me in the Students' Union elections when I stood for president, allowing my gay male friends to dress me up as Kylie for campaign posters brandishing the slogan, '*You* should be so lucky.'

As we perched on the front garden wall sharing a can of lager with Chris, he regaled us with tales of passing his annual flat inspection by gluing tufts of carpet back over plentiful cigarette burns. The landlord was oblivious to the furry Honey Monster feet he'd acquired by picking up this excess fluff. Laughing along with them, I contemplated Alice's androgynous outfit of combat pants and Converse baseball boots and wondered where her mum had got the idea that little femme me was the real gay one who had corrupted her daughter.

The area was typical of London's personality disorder at the time, during the early stages of regeneration. Stroud Green Road was the main artery running from the grimy pubs packed with Arsenal fans near the Tube towards the aloof leafiness of Crouch End. Street after street of converted Victorian terraces fanned from this route, like the veins delivering this north London suburb its life. Our flat was staggering distance from Finsbury Park itself, which hosted gigs including the annual festival of Irish music, the Fleadh.

For Alice and me, moving in with a girlfriend was an exciting first attempt at some kind of adulthood. I had finally found a teammate who wanted to engage with life head on, unlike the zombies who packed themselves into the Tube for the daily commute. We were different. We were alive. We were building a world together. It was the first time I'd had my own home to put my stamp on instead of having to confine my identity to a room in a house-share.

We limbered up for our flat-warming with a few vodkas… and then a few more vodkas, soundtracked by the fizzing chorus of Puressence's 'This Feeling'. I had invited a lot of my new contacts in journalism to the party, having decided that writing about music would go well with creating and performing it. However I was already so wasted before any of them arrived that professional networking would be something of a stretch. This was unusual behaviour for a control freak like me.

Later, I went to the bathroom and decided to undress completely… except for an unbuttoned shirt hanging loosely around my shoulders. I adopted a louche pose in the doorway, spouting some gibberish about being a butterfly emerging free from its chrysalis. The albums editor of the

NME was among those who turned to look, a mix of horror and bemusement etched onto their faces. Alice strolled nonchalantly through this gathering and buttoned my shirt up again. My protector and hero, she could sense that I would regret this. We always looked out for one another.

'Nothing to see here!' she beamed.

'Give her enough elastic and she'll always come back,' imparted one sober voice, as if this had turned into a bizarrely public couple-counselling session.

Alice and my exuberant former guitarist Debbie spent the remainder of the evening chasing me around with towels to try and cover my semi-nakedness with a kind of impromptu toga.

Debbie's presence meant that erstwhile drummer Lisa was absent. An all-female band line-up had disintegrated as rapidly as New Labour's feel-good factor when Debbie fell madly in love with the mysterious, charismatic long-haired woman behind the kit. They ended up throwing footwear at one another. Doc Martens I assume, as the result had been Lisa sustaining a broken nose. I didn't want to take sides, especially as I was a little in love with Lisa too. She had that knack of making you feel like you were the only person in the room... before moving on to the next person. Whenever Alice and I played a game of 'Would you forgive me if I accidentally snogged person X?', Lisa was pretty much always our 'person X'. She was exactly the sort of dangerous seductress we could both easily imagine behaving foolishly with in a drunkenly-charged moment. She was our free pass.

She'd already become something of a mythical figure, as significant in our world as Elvis. Even in her absence, she seemed to dominate conversation. One party guest reported a sighting of her. I felt a fleeting sobering pang of hurt that, despite my best efforts to remain a good platonic friend among a sea of women and men falling at her feet, I too had been dropped.

As the hubbub receded and stragglers drained the last bottles of nastily-coloured alcopop that had been rejected earlier in the evening, I dozed off in the spare room. I woke in the early hours, parched and confused, then staggered into the main bedroom. Alice was passed out in our bed face down, with Debbie huddled against her in a somewhat possessive and amorous pose.

'Ahem! I'm getting in now!' I announced.

Alice stirred then did a double take and released a horrified mini-scream as she realised that the body pressed close to hers wasn't mine. It wasn't absolutely clear quite what had been going on. But Alice and I had a deep mutual trust, our relaxed physical boundaries a tribute to the loving friendship we knew underpinned us. The odd lapse was fine, particularly when we were both too drunk really to know what had happened. Perhaps if there was ever a more explicit confession it would be different. But for now, we were rock solid and life was one big party. I got in between the two of them and the three of us went to sleep.

CHAPTER 2

A NEW FAMILY

My old band line-up had formed organically after we met at some auditions for a play about a female rock group. So, once that fell apart, I didn't have a sense of how best to pull a new, cohesive group of musicians together. In the meantime, I put myself forward for solo gigs, working up from two song 'floor-spots' to fuller sets. One of the most prestigious was in the cabaret tent at Pride on Clapham Common.

For the first time, a security fence was erected around the site and an admission charge was introduced, signs of the growing commercialization of the gay scene. Yet I managed to skip this with a casual wave and a camp 'I'm a performer, darling.'

I'm not sure the programmer knew what he was doing as he had booked me, an unknown, to follow immediately after

Labi Siffre of 'Something Inside So Strong' fame. Frustratingly, Alice was away and unable to look on supportively when my performance was marred by the mic stand drooping during my first song to such an extent that I almost finished it on my knees.

'It's not very erect, is it?' I quipped, the first in what became a tradition of between-song barbs that I would use to save the situation when the music aspect of the gig had gone awry.

I trudged miserably towards the exit gate during Jimmy Somerville's set. Spotting an ex-fling in a passionate embrace only served to heighten my sense of isolation. I resentfully remembered how I had ruined my *A-Z* for her, ripping out the page on which she lived so that I could carry it around in my pocket unencumbered by the whole book. I had clearly anticipated a longer relationship. As if providing a soundtrack exclusively for me, Jimmy launched into 'Don't Leave Me This Way'.

I was pretty clear that I didn't want to make music on my own. I wanted to find some new soulmates to share the highs and lows with. Heading home on the Northern line, I vowed to place an ad in the 'Musicians Wanted' column in brightly-coloured free ads newspaper *Loot*. It caught the eye of smiley curly-haired guitarist Matt, then assured and experienced bass player Dave and, finally, accident-prone yet talented drummer Simon.

To play your own music with someone you need to show

them a piece of your soul. You need to fall in love a little bit. This was harder for me to do with men, yet not impossible. In fact, maybe music would be my one true connection with men. Since coming out, I'd subconsciously filtered them out of my social life and was starting to understand the frustrating limitations that imposed on your place and context in the world.

To even up the gender balance in the band, Alice started adding backing harmonies and playing shaker on several songs. Rather than just a random way to involve my girlfriend, our vocal arrangements were starting to be part of the trademark sound. Not only that, her people skills acted as the glue that bonded our musical family together. I entrusted her with important decisions about where we played, what we wore, which songs we included in the set list, appointing her as a sort of ad hoc manager. Before long, I was incapable of making any career-related choices at all without consulting her first. She embraced how useful this made her feel.

Gloriously carefree, Alice would occasionally sleep off a clubbing session under a bench in Leicester Square before rolling into work. When I proudly unveiled a new song, 'Underachievers of the World Unite', loosely inspired by her, she felt spurred to seek a job more in keeping with her considerable intelligence and became an unlikely career woman. Her look changed accordingly, the bright orange stripes replaced by a dark Nana Mouskouri bob and severe, thick-rimmed specs. She referred to them as her 'late-night Channel-4 lesbian-debate glasses'. Longer hours meant that 'fun' Alice was less available to me. Impromptu treats, like champagne and strawberries in Soho on weekday lunchtimes, were no longer possible.

My own job at *Time Out* involved compiling coherent music listings from the faxes that spewed relentlessly from the machine. These were filed alphabetically according to venue. So entries for the Acoustic Café would often be way more thoroughly checked than those for Subterranea or The Twelve Bar Club. The latter seedy dive on Denmark Street, Soho's 'Tin Pan Alley' of guitar shops and piss smells, was the setting for our first band gig and became a regular booking.

The building was originally constructed as a stable in 1635 then converted into a forge, the disused fireplace at the rear of the stage creating a perfect cubby hole for Matt's guitar amp. For the performer, the layout felt odd. Standing on the quirkily high stage, you towered above the people on the lower level and were in turn towered over by the people on the balcony, with their feet tapping away at your eye level. The platform itself was so tiny that we could barely all squeeze on.

Matt was working full-time and feeling the effects of multiple demands on his time and energy. For him, as for Alice, a new shorter haircut reflected a new seriousness. He dozed in the redundant hours between soundcheck and gig in a cushion-decorated alcove to the left of the main balcony. He was disturbed by Alice swooping in brandishing a brown paper bag full of cheeseburgers that she'd thoughtfully bought for hungry band members, her long oversized coat flowing behind her like a superhero's cape.

'There's no way I'll ever get to play good cop now,' I sighed to myself, just a tiny bit resentfully. Her constant generosity was so lavish that it was impossible to compete. The boys all adored her... whereas they viewed me as more of a strict 'teacher' figure who had to keep them all in line.

During the performance, Alice kept a glass of wine, or several, hidden on a secret ledge just above our heads. She had a generous glug between songs, the start of a growing problem I hadn't yet noticed.

'What are you doing?' I said the next morning as she went straight to pour a large measure of brandy.

'Just getting breakfast!'

I shrugged and ate my cereal. This was the 1990s, we were in our twenties, and it seemed perfectly acceptable.

CHAPTER 3
NO SIBLINGS, NO WINGS...
GROWING UP SUCKS

Looking back now, I can see that while Jen may not have done drinking, drugs or partying to anything like the excess that Alice did, there was one big parallel between the two relationships: I looked to both to fill the void in my life, the thing that had set me apart since early childhood.

'When are my brothers and sisters coming?' I asked my parents urgently, standing in our hallway in my pyjamas.

Having their undivided attention had been good for a while. But now I felt lonely and wanted another little person knocking around. Inherited intelligence was only really useful if I had a captive audience closer to my own age to test my stories and brilliant ideas out on. All the other children at school and in the neighbourhood had siblings. Nobody was an only child. It just wasn't normal in the 1980s.

'Oh, I don't think they are coming,' said Mum, taking a crestfallen me by the hand and leading me to my bedroom. Already in her forties, she was an untypically old mother, another thing that marked us out as odd.

The previous night I'd asked when my wings were going to grow, expecting them to unfurl from my shoulder blades... perhaps when I hit my tenth birthday. I was getting a bit sick of asking grown-ups about important things. They were always full of disappointing news.

***

When I was very little, I spent part of every week living at my Auntie Ruth's. Mum was busy, having returned to work as a lecturer. Auntie Ruth was a full-time mum, with four sons. Temporarily, then, I had four big brothers. Chris, the closest to me in age, was the coolest with posters of The Jam adorning his walls. Yet it was quieter John who allowed this annoying chatterbox baby girl cousin to camp out in his room. He told me stories and entertained me with shadow puppets long after we'd been instructed to go to sleep. Philip and Nicholas seemed practically ancient and close to being adults themselves. Yet they all had the coolest toys... guns, Subbuteo and Scalextric. No wonder I felt bereft on returning home to my parents, a cuddly Snoopy and an abandoned doll. This sense of loss was a constant companion through adolescence and into my twenties. So, yes, Alice and Jen, women that I cared for and felt I had lots in common with, both had two utterly conflicting roles projected onto them... lover *and* sister.

This was the sexual blackmail at the heart of my problem with monogamy. The only way I could see that society would allow me to choose myself a sibling and recreate anything like the closeness of growing up together was to be in a relationship. You can't ask people to be your sister or brother. It's just not normal. Yet it's perfectly commonplace to ask someone you feel drawn to out on a date, even if, under the surface, it feels like the most incestuous thing in the world.

It's no surprise, then, that my sisterly relationships with Alice and Jen were punctuated by my highly charged, heart-breakingly attritional romance with Sarah and intense, short-lived passionate flings like my snogging relationship with Nat. There was no way, in a monogamous society, to fulfil both the need for companionship and the need for drama and passion simultaneously. It was a stark binary choice. The only way to cope, without cheating, was to alternate.

Each time things would start well as the grief I felt for the part I'd been missing for a few years would subside. Relief would flood through me. 'I am sexy, thank god.' But then the grief for the other half of me that I'd newly sacrificed would kick in. 'I am sexy but alone, goddammit'.

Qazi thinks however, that my craving for a 'sister' figure isn't so much about my being an only child as a narrative I've told myself to compartmentalise the two very different types of love that we *all* crave, whether we have siblings or not. He says, 'the difference you are describing is simply between the two competing relationship desires we all possess in our modular, and often conflicting, minds. That is, the one which is about passion and sex and the other that wants a trusting bond and commitment with a partner. People will differ in how much these components compete. Alternating between relationships that are either sexual or companionate is simply your modular mind flipping from one to the other.'

Qazi's description of the modular mind makes me picture my brain as a house with the different types of love represented by the distinct rooms. To date, I've struggled to find anyone I can comfortably wander around the whole house with. So we either stay stranded in domesticity in the kitchen or in shallow, hungry lust in the bedroom. It would surely take a feat of quantum physics to be able to co-exist in two or more states (or rooms) simultaneously. Being both sexy *and* steadfast is as mind-bendingly tricky as Schrödinger's cat being both dead and alive. Yet if the rooms in my house are populated by different people, I can see a way of moving between them and exploring different facets of my personality. In other words, I can see how some people would arrive at polyamory as a logical solution.

When I've discussed this dilemma with other friends in companionate relationships, they certainly seem to face the same challenges. Yet it's hard to determine how robust their anecdotal evidence is and whether they are really as binary as I seem to be. 'We never have sex' might really mean 'we only have sex once a month'. It's not like I'm hiding in their bedrooms collecting 'hard' (!) data.

However universal this 'modular mind' puzzle is, mine seems to have played out particularly destructively. I have veered from one extreme to the other and ultimately, in 2015, had returned to my strongest need for permanence, the quality I associated with 'family'.

That yearning may well have contributed to my desire the previous year to get the transient 'sex' part of the relationship 'over with' once and for all. As far as I knew, there was no permanence to physical intimacy. But 'family' was different.

Jen had made it perfectly clear from day one that she did not want children. This was fine by me. The hormonal pang for a baby that had swelled inside me during my mid-thirties, when I was trapped deep in the impossibility of love with Sarah and consequently unable to do anything about it, had passed.

Jen and I sought out a cat to complete our unit instead. Far from being a child substitute, I saw animals as pretty superior beings. Alice and I had once taken in musically-named teeny-tiny kittens, Dusty and Ella. Yet that felt so long ago. Having a pet again would just be *awesome*.

When we noticed a Facebook post about an abandoned young, white and tabby wandering hungrily around Stoke Newington, we immediately messaged, though we couldn't pick her up right away. We were due to go to Green Man Festival for me to perform in the Einstein's Gardens area. Fortunately, a cat fosterer was happy to take Lily to the vets to be spayed and to look after her for a few days while she recuperated. We spent most of our weekend in Wales at the Pets At Home superstore excitedly buying blankets, cat beds, toys and treats.

When we arrived at fosterer Jackie's house, she had cats in every corner: under the sofa, in the wardrobe and under the bed. She pointed out all these hidey-holes... 'There's Betty... Alan's living in this drawer...' We couldn't even see most of the cats she assured us were there. In discreet whispers, while Jackie made a cup of tea, we pondered if some of them were fictional, along with the 'husband' she mentioned.

Lily was camping out in her shower cubicle, a terrified scrap of fur. Jen was peering around the corner and couldn't yet see her. I made a squeezing motion with my hands to indicate that our new pet was both tiny and adorable. I felt a rush of connection with her. We were going to take care of this little creature.

Lily represented our reason to stay together, our permanence.

CHAPTER 4
END OF A CENTURY

The shift in tone away from euphoric British optimism towards the end of the 1990s was perhaps best soundtracked by Pulp's, and particularly Jarvis Cocker's, evolution from the chirpy, cheeky 'chip shops and cider' vibe of *Different Class* to the altogether bleaker, darker *This Is Hardcore*. In my *Time Out* column, I noted that 'our geeky hero' had started to 'question the meaning of fame'. I too was distilling an emerging sense of unease into my own music, with the chorus of one new song proclaiming, 'this love is doomed.' Whoa! What dark part of my subconscious had *that* come from? It seemed cruel to ask Alice to sing backing vocals on it. Yet it really was a great song.

'The girls would love to see you. Why don't you come with me?' she asked one warm Sunday morning, standing on our front drive opening the car door.

I was awkwardly hopping from one foot to the other as I hadn't put any shoes on.

'No, I think I'll stay here and finish my new song,' I said, unconvincingly.

'Are you sure? Come on, come and have a Bloody Mary and a Stilton burger.'

'No, I'm alright. I'll see you tonight.'

The dynamic of dependence that we had created had eroded my confidence. I was becoming more reclusive. I only wanted to go out with Alice if I felt reassured that I could be her sole focus. When she was with her gang, I felt excluded, confined to the sidelines. The way that Alice's straight, girly mates processed the relationship was to view me as one of the 'boyfriends'. This gender-bending, distant identity was reinforced by the way that they tended to address me as 'Wilby', the surname-only moniker I used as an artist.

It seemed unfair. I had opened up my world and life to Alice, allowing her pole position within the inner sanctum of the band. Yet while my friends had become 'our' friends, it felt very much like her friends remained hers. Maybe it was my fault. Maybe I hadn't made a big enough effort. I didn't have the answer.

Alice's family was equally tough to gatecrash my way into, despite her huge efforts to come out to them all. Three portly protective elder brothers all looked mafia-esque in the photos I'd seen, ready to kill any man who mistreated their baby sis. Yet what were they supposed to say to a female partner?

'I like you Rosie, but...' mused the eldest quizzically over dinner in Islington, 'you're shagging my sister!'

'Yes,' I nodded, telepathically urging Alice to get back from the toilets quickly.

Her mum pleaded, 'Don't tell your father, it'll upset him.'

Yet as it turned out, he was the least perturbed by the news. 'Well... knock me over with a feather,' he beamed, before hugging his daughter and pouring them both a large brandy. He quickly became the one that I felt most comfortable around.

Even while I was retreating into shyness and insecurity, Alice's immensely social nature, coupled with the openness of our hedonistic early days, robbed us of the privacy around our relationship that I was now craving.

'Let's have a Saturday night in all to ourselves,' she stated with intent one unusually empty, rehearsal-free weekend.

'Oh God, yes please!' I beamed.

No sooner had we slid Jeff Buckley's *Grace* into the CD player than we heard a pitiful, timid knock at the door. Upstairs neighbour Chris had been dumped by his girlfriend and stood clutching four cans of lager, tentatively inviting himself in. After an hour of conversation, it was clear he wasn't going back upstairs.

Alice clapped her hands decisively together, 'Right! We're all going to go clubbing at G-A-Y.'

Resolutely-straight Chris seemed a little uneasy and I wondered if Alice had suggested such a queer-sounding outing to shake him off. However, he agreed and we all bundled into a taxi to the Astoria. Several beers into the evening he boasted, 'I've had my arse pinched by two different men!'

Alice and I played our regular game of seeing who could chat up the most attractive woman and get her to join us for drinks.

'Let's see what you come back with,' I said rather un-encouragingly when it was her turn to go off and scour the crowd. The trouble with G-A-Y was that many of the women were straight fag hags and not there to be flirted with by lesbians looking to spice up their relationship. We usually ended up with confused Spanish tourists who didn't speak great English but might at least dance with us for a little while.

Alice disappeared for an hour as she drunkenly stumbled onstage with some drag queens, an unofficial additional part of the entertainment. Chris and I peered down from the balcony above, smiling at her impressive nonchalance. When we finally found her again and got ourselves home, Alice and I tumbled into bed.

'So... where were we?' I asked, as we had a playful snog.

'Ha ha, yeah,' she replied, 'before we were interrupted...'

We kissed a bit more yet neither of us could keep our eyes open.

'Goodnight,' I murmured, as I turned away from her to sleep.

CHAPTER 5

MUM

In September, three days before my twenty-ninth birthday, I was engrossed in the highlights of a US Open tennis match between Greg Rusedski and Todd Martin. Rusedski was throwing away his opportunities. He was a frustrating player to support, and not even properly British, but I still preferred him to weedy Tim Henman.

Alice was visiting her family. Her mum was getting used to the idea that we were a couple but, that day, I had made my regular excuse of finishing off demos of new songs. Normally, I'd wander Finsbury Park for inspiration then get out my guitars, keyboard and four-track recorder. But this particular weekend I couldn't focus on writing and was distracted by the tennis.

I almost didn't hear the phone, but rushed to the desk in the spare room when its nagging and prolonged ring alerted me to the fact that this was someone who really wanted to get through. It was a nurse from the cancer hospice in Southport.

'Your mum's here with us at the moment and we think you should come up right away,' she said, as sweetly as she could while also impressing on me the urgency of the matter.

I couldn't understand it. I wasn't even sure I knew Mum was *in* a hospice. My parents had never openly discussed her illness with me. Perhaps it was out of a sense of protection, yet the awful truth was that it meant that I hadn't been preparing for this.

'You mean...' I stumbled, my knee bashing against the office chair and causing it to swivel and squeak, thinking of how on earth to say the unsayable. 'She's getting... worse?'

I'd seen Mum only a fortnight earlier and she'd seemed alright, albeit thin, driving herself off to the shops and to go birdwatching at Martin Mere. Dad and I had strolled together through the local fields. He hadn't given me any indication that I needed to stay close.

I'd even witnessed a new tenderness between my parents, he occasionally touching her cheek. Now I wondered if it was to imprint the memory of her face before it faded away. I had felt soothed in the knowledge that they did really love each other, despite all those years of separate cars and plans on holidays. Yet something had gone terribly wrong. She'd deteriorated after deciding to stop treatment.

She had always erred on the side of less, rather than more,

medical attention. She had once removed me from the orthodontist's chair at a Southport clinic, unwilling to put me through unnecessary discomfort and operations. She was right. Wonky teeth wouldn't kill me. Yet this *was* something that was going to kill her. And she'd had enough of fighting it.

A memory came to me... a letter she'd sent a few months earlier inside a card with a painting on the front... of bluebells in some woods, maybe. She had been trying to tell me something, perhaps even to say goodbye. I'd been reading it on the bus and felt queasy so stowed it away deep in the bottom of my cavernous bag, among collapsed parts of old broken biros and out-of-date Travelcards. I hadn't wanted to digest the message.

I wasn't sure how I was supposed to feel. Abandoned, perhaps? Weren't a few more months or years with Dad and me worth fighting for? There was no point in thinking that now, and no time. If I wanted to see her again, I had to act quickly.

I tried Alice's phone. It was switched off. I pictured her in her parents' extensive garden playing with her niece and nephews, a bittersweet image given that my own family was about to shrink unthinkably. When we eventually spoke, she had just arrived back at the flat and I was already on the train to Liverpool in a daze.

'Didn't you leave the keys for me under the mat like we said?' she asked, rummaging around for them.

'Oh …' I mumbled, suddenly remembering that she'd not been able to find hers that morning, 'I'm sorry… I forgot.'

Yet sensing my numbness at the other end of the phone, she realised something more important was wrong, something less fixable.

'Don't worry, I'll call a locksmith... Are you alright?'

'I don't know... I'll call you later.'

I didn't have a bag, a coat, or anything with me and tried, for the only time in my life ever, to read the Virgin train magazine full of suggestions for exciting days out in Preston. I departed London without knowing what any sort of future held. What would I *need* now? I had no idea.

I sat and wrote the opening verse to the song 'Take My Hand'.

'Mother, are the demons here
To fill my heart with blood and life and fear
Why can't I stay
Here
Mother, are the demons here
To fill my mind with love and light and fear
Why can't I stay
Near'

And then there was no music, just silence... and just one parent's signature in my birthday card.

The immediate aftermath dragged by in its grim, relentless fashion. I calmly accompanied Dad to collect the death certificate and pick up a clear little plastic bag containing Mum's slippers, watch and glasses from the hospice. These were small, insubstantial artefacts yet were now all that represented her in the real world.

He asked me to phone her oldest friend Joan to deliver the awful news. 'Thanks for letting me know,' she said, in a distant, grey tone of muted devastation.

I felt peculiarly matter-of-fact, as if it was all just a dream. A surreal numbness took over. In fact, most nights I did dream that none of this was real. Waking up became a confusing limbo. For a few semi-conscious minutes each morning, I felt certain that Mum was still alive. Then I'd be shaken from this hopeful state by the sound of Dad sobbing in his bedroom below as he opened the curtains to let in another lonely day. It was the worst sound in the world.

Alice had just started a new job and was immediately forced out of the closet as she had to ask for day off to attend her partner's mother's funeral. Back then, anyone who used the word 'partner' was gay. She drove up late in the evening after work, sleeping in the car in a lay-by so as not to disturb us in the middle of the night.

Mum had become interested in Quakerism later in life so had expressed a wish for a relatively simple funeral, mostly consisting of quiet contemplation but with the chance for people to speak spontaneously if they wanted to. Joan stood up and talked about how she could sense that Mum was still present with us in some way.

She'd left a notebook of memories hurriedly written in

her distinctive spidery handwriting, a result of being forced to write right-handed at school instead of using her natural left. Dad, Alice and I started typing them up to print for close friends and family. Although difficult to read in both a practical and emotional sense, it was worth the effort. I got to know her better than I had done in her lifetime.

Despite the austerity and anxiety of the war, her nomadic childhood had been full of love, fun, bike rides and nature, broken up by her Methodist minister father's moves to a new church every five or so years. He was incredibly popular everywhere he went and I wondered whether I'd inherited some of his desire to communicate with an audience. It certainly didn't seem to come from my parents, who never seemed to embrace the performance element of teaching.

Four older brothers getting into fights and scrapes on the streets of Bootle added a frisson to Mum's early life. She often had to cover for them as they bathed battle scars and bruises. Even though the start of her education was held back a year so that she could keep her younger sister company, she was already a voracious reader, early signs of the intelligence that would eventually win her a scholarship to Girton College, Cambridge.

Although a move to Scarborough in 1938 took her away from a small private school to a much larger and scarier primary full of boisterous behaviour and nits, it was there she met her best friend Marjorie. Their famous giggling fits would often see them getting sent out of class or having to stuff hankies in their mouths at church. They even combined their names and called themselves 'Maraldene'. Marjorie ended up marrying my Uncle Henry. When she died in her fifties of a sudden heart attack in church, I hadn't understood the huge significance of this friendship and what a devastating loss it must have been. Yet knowing that my mum had such closeness with other women helped me to understand my own romantic same-sex attachments and where that could have come from.

Once I returned to Finsbury Park, I barricaded myself in the flat, spending days alone with my four-track in a creative cocoon. This self-imposed isolation was partly because I couldn't share the experience of losing a parent with any of my peers and felt more of an odd one out than ever. But it was also that the heightened stress and emotion had unlocked a strange febrile songwriting energy. I completed 'Take My Hand', with an outro that built and built a bit like Blur's 'Tender'. Music was going to be the thing that got me through. It became my obsession.

One evening, after a long day, Alice came home from work and ran us a hot bubble bath. We still made an effort to make time for each other in that early evening window before I returned to fretting about songs and gigs and she cracked open the booze. Dusty ran up to the bath, placing her front paws on the side and chirruped cheerfully, happy to see her mums together, while Ella jumped up to do a tightrope walk along the edge, leaning in to lick the drips from the tap.

Alice had a holiday booked in Buenos Aires to visit a friend who'd been posted out there with the Foreign Office.

'I could rearrange it if you need me here,' she offered.

'It's fine. You go,' I replied coldly. I rather liked the idea of being alone with my thoughts and my music with no distractions.

'You're breaking my heart,' she sobbed, her hand making a single, frustrated, gentle slap onto the frothy, viscous surface. She wanted to be needed. But, for once, she didn't know how to make everything better.

Alice and I had been thrust so rapidly from our hedonistic, carefree existence into adulthood. Perhaps it was no wonder that we had begun to unravel.

My grief for Mum was compounded by the fact that my other 'family', the band, was in crisis. Drummer Simon had grown distrustful of the Rosie-Alice power axis. His passive-aggressive method of protest was to turn up later and later. At rehearsals, this was frustrating but not deadly. Yet when we had to walk on stage at a Mean Fiddler gig without him, having received no message, phone call or apology, I felt devastatingly betrayed.

Given her informal 'manager' role, Alice tried to mediate, resolve the misunderstanding and coax him back. Yet, as a partner, I wanted her to be utterly on my side and not to try to see his. She was walking a perilous tightrope and didn't know what to do for the best. Even her mystical people skills couldn't keep things together when Matt, suffering from a combination of a broken heart and work stress, decided to follow Simon out of the band. Our dreams of collective musical adventures were collapsing into dust and escaping through my fingers too fast for me to keep hold of them.

Meanwhile, the gay community in London was starting to fragment too. A few of my favourite haunts and spiritual homes started to close down. Looking back, I can see how my quest for ersatz siblings in both the music scene and then the gay community was in direct conflict with settling into a romantic relationship.

Recently I watched the documentary *Who's Gonna Love Me Now* about a gay Israeli man, Saar. He fled the fears and prejudices of his biological family to find a host of surrogate brothers in London with the Gay Men's Chorus. A beautiful redemptive film, it prompted me to read more about what his early life would have been like in a kibbutz. Fascinatingly, three researchers had written about psychological effects of kibbutzim in the 1950s and 1960s. They all concluded that growing up in such a tightly-knit community lead to individuals having greater difficulty in forming single, strong emotional commitments yet an easier time in having larger numbers of less-involved friendships. This sounded to me exactly like the effect that immersing myself in the gay subculture of 1990s London had on me. I got to know tons of people and, on the surface, was having a brilliant time. But how many of those connections had actually reached the depth I craved and lasted through the years? Not many at all.

It was also suggested that young people from the kibbutz preferred to seek mates outside of the community. This acted as a perfect metaphor for why I'd felt so differently about Sarah from how I had about either Alice or Jen. The partner I was more romantically drawn to and sexually comfortable with was the one who was in the closet and at odds with her gayness. She wasn't part of my logical 'family'. So any taboo was lifted. It was the ultimate paradox. The thing that made the reality of a relationship impossible was the very thing that made it possible to fall in love with her.

***

'Shall we have a bath together tonight?'

It was a grey Sunday in late 2015, a boring nothing-y day. Jen was making one last stab at initiating intimacy. It seemed in direct contradiction to our discussion on the sofa a few months earlier.

Yet I missed her. Desperately. I missed giving her a kiss as she left for work. I missed gently holding her as we drifted off to sleep.

We had been so careful not to give one another mixed messages that we'd each put up separate force fields and kept a respectful distance away. Each night we pinned ourselves to the opposite sides of the king-sized bed.

I did feel happier and calmer in myself. Maybe a bath would be relatively safe. It wouldn't need to lead to anything else.

'Yeah, let's do it,' I smiled.

But the pre-planned nature of this rekindling of *something* loaded it with heavy expectation. I turned on the taps and waited for the water to warm up, feeling my passion leak away. I prepared the bath as I always had, just below my preferred temperature but cool enough for her, leaving her the less cluttered shower-free end. A few scented candles, bath salts...

As she stepped gracefully in, my familiar anxiety returned. We splashed around for a few minutes, silently.

'I'm sorry, I don't feel comfortable. It seems weird.'

'Oh.'

'You're like my sister. It doesn't feel right to be naked with you.'

It was out there. I hadn't ever said the sister thing out loud.

'Oh right,' said Jen, frowning and washing herself in a much more perfunctory and practical manner.

I got out and towelled myself down, aware that I'd just delivered the final, fatal blow to any sexual closeness we could ever have.

CHAPTER 7

MY BRILLIANT TEAM-MATE

I filled the critical twelve months following Mum's death with recording an album and making plans to release it on my own label, using a modest amount of money that she had left me. The producers, laid-back drummer Barnaby and whiskery guitarist Chris, owned a small studio in Tulse Hill and luckily filled the temporary gaps in the band line-up.

The album title *Precious Hours* was lifted from the middle-eight section of my Verve-influenced ode to ambition, 'Dreams'.

'So come on, don't let the world just turn round,
Don't let yourself down,
So come on, don't let these precious hours pass by,
All these excuses are just lies.'

Aware that life was short, I pushed forward with my career, making things happen, making sense of all the bewilderment and despair.

I received a phone call from my distributor, telling me that the album had made it on to the racks of Virgin and HMV, while pitching a tent at Glastonbury.

'Well done, babe!' Alice beamed, hammering a peg into the ground, 'Let's get champagne.'

We were squeezing into the tiniest spot pushed right up against the fence. We had left late after I'd been held up by a Jobseekers' interview. I thought they must have been suspicious about my activities and purposefully booked it for the first day of the biggest music festival of the year. Alice was always moaning about how she paid her taxes to support dole scroungers like me. Yet, in the same way that we resolved many minor niggles and disagreements, we would pour ourselves a drink and tipsily laugh away these political differences.

The weather was baking and we floated around the site on a high, handing out flyers promoting the impending album release. David Bowie was the big Sunday headliner, a gargantuan leap in class up from Saturday's amiable, yet ultimately forgettable closers, Travis. When he sauntered on with tousled long hair, wearing a Hunky Dory-esque three-quarter-length jacket, I shivered with anticipation. It was really him. He strutted through a godlike set, kicking off with a stunning 'Wild Is the Wind', shaven-headed Gail Ann Dorsey's ice-cool distinctive bass intro causing tribes of fans to press closer to the stage, shrouded by pink evening sky. After reviewing countless gigs, I'd become so critical of anything less than genius. Not many performers connected with me like this. Alice and I linked arms and sang along through anthemic classics 'Life On Mars', 'Ashes to Ashes' and 'Rebel Rebel'. There was a tangible sense of our relationship recovering from the trauma of Mum's death. We were developing a new closeness, strengthened by our survival of such a big life event and by being so energised by music.

Earlier in the day, David Gray had been promoted up to the Pyramid Stage on the back of the success of his album *White Ladder* and single 'Babylon', which he'd originally released on his own label after re-mortgaging his house. If someone as ordinary as him could make the independent route pay off, then surely so could I? I felt cautiously optimistic.

Distribution into major shops seemed like a huge victory. On the day of the release, Alice and I marched triumphantly into the flagship Virgin Megastore on Tottenham Court Road where I had once been mesmerised at a listening post for the entirety of the Kate Bush album *The Red Shoes*. We looked in the 'W' section… we saw Wilco… Kim Wilde… Robbie Williams… We were getting closer… My heart was beating a bit faster… Was it here?

No, we couldn't find it. I felt crestfallen. Alice went to ask for it at the desk as I hid behind a pillar. If it was here and they recognised me from the cover photo, it would look a little desperate to be asking for my own album. She came back from the desk beaming and giving me one of her winks. 'Don't worry,' she said, 'It'll be on the shelves tomorrow'.

We returned the next day and there was the little plastic sign with the band name Wilby punched out in white on black tape, alongside three copies of the shrink-wrapped CD. I threw my arms around her, laughing with delight, knowing I couldn't have achieved any of this without her support. We made a pretty spectacular team.

A few days later, we squeezed into the BBC London studios with Dave, his double bass and presenter Amy Lamé for a session and interview. Our rendition of 'You Amaze Me' prompted several listeners to email in.

As we walked home along Upper Tollington Park, I had a strange unsettled feeling. We turned into the drive and saw Chris standing in the doorway, an unfamiliar look of concern etched onto his face. It seemed odd. He was telling us there had been 'some kind of accident'.

CHAPTER 8
UP IN SMOKE

It took a split second to digest what he was saying. What had once been our front door was boarded up with a piece of corrugated metal. A yellow Post-it note from the Fire Brigade saying 'See you in the morning' with a time and contact number was merrily stuck in the middle at a jaunty angle, as if it were a note from a friend who'd popped round and missed us.

A fleeting memory of a happier time at that very threshold flashed jarringly through my mind. I pictured Alice falling down the stairs into a giggling heap at the bottom, like an *Ab Fab* character, as we had returned jubilantly from the Pulp and Catatonia concert in the park a couple of summers earlier.

'What about the cats?' I whispered, panic constricting my vocal chords.

Alice and Chris ran round to the back garden and found them running around confused and crying. They had survived, at least. That was something.

I longed to claw and rip away the grey makeshift hoarding and crawl into the dark abyss that our home had become. Pushing my face up to the blackened window, I was confronted with a bleak, empty blindness.

I staggered into the road, sinking into the darkness, dizzy with grief, wondering what would be salvageable, what wouldn't. We had no way of checking until the morning. Chris guided me back towards the pavement.

I sat on the front garden wall with Alice. 'Our relationship won't survive this,' I said spikily, the small volume of dusky evening air between us suddenly amplified.

'Don't say that,' she pleaded, vulnerability leaking through her ever-competent façade.

It was a surprise to find myself saying it. But it was true. The rekindling we'd begun at Glastonbury was halted in its tracks, our recovery thwarted. There was no way to navigate yet another huge loss together within a matter of months. It was just too painful. Besides, our home represented our relationship – the band, the parties, our friendship with Chris. There was something so symbolic about all of those memories drifting away across Finsbury Park in a plume of smoke.

And, perhaps most importantly, I realised that the person I'd come to delegate all my decisions to, to lean on so heavily, couldn't take care of us both. She couldn't singlehandedly keep us, the band, the cats *and* our home safe and all together. It was too much of a burden to carry for even a self-appointed 'superhero' like Alice. I'd fallen into the trap of thinking that a partner could be absolutely everything at all times. Because that was what I'd always been told to think, not least by Alice herself.

The next morning as I came to in an unfamiliar bed in Chris's spare room with Alice next to me, my first thought was that we were on holiday. I sighed contentedly, stretched out my legs and continued to doze. Just as I had in the mornings after Mum's death, I basked in the comforting warmth of a few moments of unreality before awareness set in. Alice leaned in to touch my shoulder.

'We have to phone the fire investigation team and go and meet them,' she whispered, holding the dreaded yellow note in front of my face. With that, the black knot in my stomach returned.

Once we gained access to the dank cave that our flat had become, it was a stark demonstration of how heat rises. A guitar lying flat on the floor was virtually undamaged yet the ones on stands were fine up to the neck and then completely deformed, twisted into a different instrument altogether. The keys on my keyboards had melted into strange stalactites as if stretching out, gasping for cleaner air near the floor. Clothes, pictures, letters, videos were all coated in thick black soot, fragments of our lives dirty and destroyed. The only CD that had escaped was the one stuck in my player, the first Elbow album, fittingly a resilient band who had overcome much of their own adversity.

Fortunately my own albums were still all boxed up at the other end of the flat and would be salvageable once we'd removed the blackened cardboard. The landlord's highly flammable furniture had pretty much disintegrated. Perhaps that's how we got our deposit back so quickly. He couldn't wait to claim the insurance, redecorate and hike up the rent for the next tenants.

For a few tedious few weeks, we camped around London, flat-sitting for various holidaying friends, peppered with sad trips up to Finsbury Park to clean up and sort through our remaining possessions. Sometimes we cried a little in the car outside, as if visiting a grave.

The cats lived wild in the back garden for days, Chris feeding them, before a comical herding session allowed us to crowbar them into their boxes and pop them in the car to join our travelling circus.

My album launch gig was booked in at Camden Monarch the following week. The timing was less than ideal. But there was no way I was cancelling. Alice and I stood side by side, dressed head-to-toe in clothes donated by sympathetic friends. We gazed into one another's eyes as we sang the optimistic chorus of 'This Time': 'I won't let it get the better of me and you'. In that fleeting, precious moment, under the warm glow of stage lights and in front of a supportive audience, our love felt invincible again. It was like we were back at Glastonbury watching Bowie.

We couldn't continue our rootless existence, however. So the issue of where we were going to live loomed large. Alice's parents came down to London to view an ex-council flat in Nunhead that they were going to help her to buy, before taking us out for a curry in East Dulwich.

We'd both been sorting through our damaged possessions at the old flat that afternoon, so were dirty and dishevelled. I felt confused as to where I fitted into the whole financial arrangement and was barely eating or saying much. Alice sensed this so followed me to the toilets, took my hand and looked me firmly in the eyes.

'Marry me,' she whispered, hopefully.

She'd always taken on the role of solving everything. Yet this seemed too much chaos even for her to smooth over with her trademark charm, champagne and flowers. The cramped hand basin area at Mirash Tandoori with her parents just the other side of a flimsy door was hardly the location I'd dreamed of for my first proposal. I could barely breathe, acutely aware that we had to rejoin the dinner table as if things were normal. Would we *celebrate* this desperate attempt to salvage our broken lives?

No. I couldn't do it. A look between us, soot-stained and sad, meant that we both knew our relationship, like most of our stuff, was toast.

CHAPTER 9

SHOULD I HAVE SAID YES?

I know you're thinking it. Alice, and my relationship with her, sound pretty cool, don't they? Many, many times I've wondered if that proposal was a 'sliding door' moment. And maybe I made the wrong choice.

Perhaps if we hadn't been kyboshed by the fire so soon after Mum's death, we would have stayed together for at least a few more years. I would have escaped all the heartache of my relationship with Sarah. Maybe.

Yet the problem with settling into a first serious relationship is that we have no idea how good we have it. There's nothing to compare it to. We don't realise that other potential partners might, in reality, be even worse and even more annoying than our current one. We arrogantly assume that we will always be able to trade up. Without that knowledge, we chase our tails in ever-decreasing circles.

Once you've left one good relationship, a life of rapid serial monogamy probably follows.

Let's not forget, though, that Alice and I couldn't legally have married in 2000. That was still a spooky sci-fi pipe-dream. Even civil partnerships hadn't arrived yet. So I'm not sure I know exactly what she meant by 'marry me'. I assume we would have had some kind of celebration (another party, yay!) and got together whatever legal paperwork we could to demonstrate our commitment. But I know in my heart that we still would have ended. I had a restlessness that I didn't fully acknowledge at the time yet which seeped out constantly in yearning, lusty song lyrics. Even though it was counter to my best interests, I was already searching for a 'Sarah', someone to fulfil more of a romantic fantasy role than the jovial 'partner-in-crime' role that Alice occupied. And, fluid as our boundaries were, we certainly knew nothing about the concept of open relationships. The temporary jealousies that flared up after we separated make me pretty certain we could never have navigated anything like that.

Perhaps more importantly, I was looking for someone who would allow me to take charge. That would have never happened with Alice. Long before those two big tragic events happened, I had disempowered myself. Alice's big, fun personality wasn't always easy to be around. I was engulfed by it. I only really started to define myself in the years after we separated. I made some terrible misjudgements. But they were essential ones. I learned from them. If I'd said yes, I would never have started comedy or written this book.

So, no, much as it's tempting to berate my younger self, I don't think I should have said yes. But would I say yes now if someone with as much wit, intelligence and loyalty asked me? Well, that's the big question.

I have such a tricky relationship with the concept of marriage. Many of my coolest, feminist straight friends have circumvented the whole idea, thinking it too patriarchal and archaic. Instead, they prefer to co-habit and would happily have civil partnerships if they were available to them.

As more and more gay friends have posted engagements on Facebook these past few years, each has been a psychological blow. The only chance I had ever had to do what they were doing was the best part of twenty years ago. I was relieved to always be busy on tour for all the weddings. I even missed my good friend Rachel's ceremony. Yet sometimes I feel bored of being angry. And wonder if I might quite like to say yes if the right person came along.

PART 4

HOW I GOT OUT OF THIS MESS...

AND WHAT I ENDED UP THINKING ABOUT RELATIONSHIPS

CHAPTER 1

2015:

MARRIED AT FIRST SIGHT

'There's no way I'd ever do it,' said Jen.

'Hmmm, I don't know,' I replied. 'If there's anything I trust at all, it's science.'

We were stretched out on our sofa, Lily curled up on a cushion asleep between us, watching the first episode of Channel 4's *Married at First Sight*. It had become a rare thing for us to engage with the same programme, our divergent tastes illustrated by the confused extremes of our shared Netflix account. Recently-watched lists were a strange amalgam of my twisty thrillers and dramas and her comedy and current affairs. Yet the premise of this show had piqued a curiosity in both of us.

Surely it was a sign of just how difficult it had become to meet someone that even affluent, attractive people were turning to reality TV for help, willing to tie the knot with a complete stranger under the full glare of cameras and lights. Trusting an app algorithm to deliver up our best romantic options is one thing. But now it seemed that sane human beings were absenting themselves from the decision-making process altogether. I wondered if it was an indication of just how much we had lost faith in our pesky, conflicting, modular minds.

In 2010, the Office of National Statistics reported that the marriage rate in England and Wales had plummeted to its lowest level since records began in 1862. Could this televised form of extreme, sudden-death dating become matrimony's unlikely saviour? Would audiences swoon and be seduced by the idea of a lifelong legal commitment, mentally signing themselves up for the next series... Or were we simply hoping to gloat as a compelling emotional car crash unfolded in front of us?

'She's gorgeous!' I exclaimed, as a dark-haired woman called Kate appeared onscreen, explaining how a hectic schedule didn't allow for the demands of dating. Jen murmured her agreement, as we watched Kate and her potential husbands go through a series of DNA and psychometric tests – answering questionnaires, spitting into tubes, being measured in every dimension.

Evolutionary anthropologist Anna Machin was part of the panel tasked with matching the perfect couple, through factors including facial symmetry and genotyping. She explained that meeting someone face-to-face and looking

284

into their eyes, as opposed to communicating online via an app or dating site, would produce a way bigger hit of the bonding chemical, oxytocin, and so she felt there might be a chance of a more romantic-feeling initial connection than one facilitated by an exchange of messages.

Also on the five-strong matching team was psychosexual relationship therapist Jo Coker, who explored past relationship histories and attitudes to sex and family. She was due to work with the couples after they had married. I couldn't help but think she might have a tough job ahead.

Kate's first glance at her equally-attractive new husband Jason as they exchanged vows seemed unexpectedly romantic. They instinctively held hands. Parents and on-looking friends smiled.

'I think they really do fancy each other,' I said.

'Yeah,' concurred Jen, 'they look a bit similar. So maybe...'

Perhaps this freakish experiment had worked, and all the anticipation and mystery had built up to this moment of falling in love at the altar.

However, less than a fortnight after the wedding, Jason was caught using Tinder by one of Kate's friends. In a meeting with the show's resident Reverend, Nick Devenish, they annulled the partnership. Even the only couple, Emma and James, who were still together as the series ended, called it a day after eight-and-a-half months. The TV narrative, contrived or not, had reinforced my thinking that attraction was not a reliable enough basis on which to make decisions about whom we share a mortgage and home with. And, as much as the participants had wanted to entrust themselves to the panel, perhaps Big Brother selecting a mate for us is just too alienating.

'If I could, I'd marry you,' I stated boldy, as the credits rolled.

Jen laughed. She thought I was joking.

But I was deadly serious. It was the most rational decision I could make. I loved living with her. I trusted and respected her. I was getting to understand the world she worked in and getting to know and like some of her colleagues. We both adored Lily. Being with Jen made sense and felt safe, whereas sex and romance really didn't. Believing in those concepts had amounted to one big, heart-breaking let down.

Yet a platonic union simply wasn't allowed, even by the activists and agitators who had vociferously campaigned for 'marriage equality'. Exchanging lifelong vows with a partner was less available to *me* than it had ever been, because marriage, in our modern Western world at least, was now so narrowly and short-sightedly defined as a romantic-only construct.

It seemed a great irony that the queer community, who had long found their own alternatives to mainstream social norms, were now the ones embracing all the very worst old traditions. A friend of mine had a hen night and allowed herself to be decorated in neon pink accessories and penis boppers. I made my escape to the toilets while these were being handed out. 'Why has it come to this?' I raged, as I hid for as long as politely possible.

If I ever do have a wedding of my own, I reckon it would be more appropriate to be given away by a procession of ex-partners than by my dad. Let's face it, that's the real 'handover' that's taking place.

In March 2014, just ahead of the first same-sex marriages in the UK, I wrote an opinion piece for the website *When Sally Met Sally* arguing that the change in the law could actually be *bad* news for lesbians. If we followed our natural patterns of relatively rapid serial monogamy, then 'we are all going to be paying for several divorces in our lifetimes,' I wrote. What's more, we might feel like our relationships were 'failing' by normative standards. Would it be worth considering open partnerships, as gay men had done, as a way of making our primary relationships last longer? Needless to say, the article ruffled a few feathers and made me a little bit unpopular with my lesbian friends who were planning a wedding.

One common argument against ethically open or poly marriages is that they might, in some way, mess up the children if their parents are off gallivanting with a different lover every night. But, in one documentary about a poly family that I saw, the kids were all having a great time, with multiple half-siblings around to play with and lots of 'mums' to give them the attention and care they needed. I would have given anything to have had that much stimulation and fun in my childhood. Meanwhile, the group of wives positively relished one another's companionship and the extra hands on deck to share domestic tasks. By contrast, the sole man seemed a little frazzled.

After discovering an article by twenty-two-year-old London-based writer Benedict Smith about growing up in a poly household, I ended up in an email chat with him. He said, 'Mum might have had up to four partners at a time. Dad had partners too.' These interconnected relationships were committed for decades. The situation was explained to him at eight years old and didn't worry him in the slightest. He described it as 'mind-numbingly ordinary' and that it simply meant 'more love and support' and more adults to look after him and his brother. 'Good parents are good parents, whether there are one or two or three or four of them. Fortunately, mine were incredible.'

He now considers himself open to either having multiple partners or just one.

CHAPTER 2
WHAT DO WE CALL EACH OTHER NOW?

'I told one person you were my ex,' mused Jen, sipping her coffee, 'but that didn't seem quite right.'

'I know!' I replied. 'I said that once but knew it was totally the wrong word. When I'm talking to poly people who get it, I say that you're my platonic partner or platonic primary. But most people won't understand that.'

Our relationship was invisible because there wasn't a recognised *word* for it. It was so disempowering not having any way to declare it. If only we had all the definitions of love that the Greeks had – *eros* (romantic, erotic), *ludus* (flirting), *philia* (shared experience), *philautia* (self-respect), *pragma* (enduring love), *storge* (family love) and *agape* (love of humanity). I suppose *storge* was the closest.

We were having brunch together in Herne Hill. Things had moved on a stage for us. After a year of flu, colds, migraines and a vomiting cat, we had become too restless each night to continue sharing a bed. So Jen had ordered a futon for the room downstairs and moved out of the main bedroom into our office.

I wondered how many couples broke up because they were just *too tired* and not getting enough uninterrupted sleep? My emotional exhaustion had been illustrated one morning as I put away the shopping delivery and dropped a full bottle of red wine. It smashed across the floor, oozing blood-like into the cracks between the tiles.

'For fuck's sake,' I shouted.

'It's only a bottle of wine,' sighed Jen. 'It wasn't even that expensive.'

But now that exhaustion was over. A new sense of calm permeated the house. After eighteen months of sharing our expensive, comfy bed, it was pure ecstasy to have it to myself. I sighed with satisfaction every night as I stretched out into the acres of soft white sheets, the full duvet, the best pillows. Even the occasional nocturnal bite from Lily couldn't dent my feelings of jubilation. I could watch TV or read emails until whatever time I wanted, eat late-night sugary snacks, fart, snore and masturbate to my heart's content.

If the relationship was a complex, chess-like strategic game, I had been propelled from a losing to winning status overnight. I felt transformed by the untying of this final knot in the sleeves of my emotional straitjacket. I was beginning to feel deeply happy and settled sharing my home with Jen, now that we had begun to redefine 'us'. All the anxiety, panic attacks and nightmares of a few years earlier had subsided. The clouds had parted and the fog lifted. I was enjoying my work and my friends. I had finally got what I wanted and extricated myself Houdini-like from the exclusive romantic pact that I had never even been aware I had signed up to in the first place.

We were both tentatively using dating apps, now that we could more legitimately say that we were 'friends' who lived together and were both 'single'. We hadn't directly discussed seeing new people in anything other than very hypothetical terms.

'If I met someone, I wouldn't bring them back here,' we agreed.

It never seemed real. I just didn't really feel attracted to anyone. I loved having the possibility of dating and sex dangling there temptingly. But I realised more and more that, now I had my psychological space and freedom *as well as* a domestic situation that suited me, I didn't mind not acting on it. Celibacy wasn't so bad at all if there was nobody there in the bed that you felt you *should* be having sex with.

Then, one day, I opened up Jen's laptop to do some audio editing and saw *Guardian* Soulmates among her frequently visited sites. She was out for drinks with work colleagues that evening. From my bedroom upstairs, I listened out for her key in the front door. It was relief to hear her come in. Sometime in the near future, she might be out all night. I didn't want to face that possibility just *yet*.

I hadn't bothered with registering and paying on Soulmates. A cursory search of available left-wing gay women in the right age bracket produced a long list of people I already knew. It was a small world. If I was going to find somebody outside of my extensive social circle, she would probably have to be a *Daily Mail* reader.

It was one early December morning during these ambiguous post-romantic months that Facebook decided to stage its own intervention and became an unlikely truth-teller, puncturing my peace. I'd been on one of my rather pathetic runs around Brockwell Park, which always involved more stopping to stroke cute dogs than actual sprinting. The weather was so unusually mild that I'd been brave enough to wear shorts. Back at home, I sat on the stairs panting and sweating and reached for my iPad.

I barely checked Facebook. So why I did that day I don't know. I had reached my maximum five-thousand 'friends', which surely says more than anything about how the currency of that particular word has been shot to pieces. Every birthday, hundreds of strangers sent well wishes.

'I can't believe I haven't seen you for a year,' said one.

'I can,' I thought, 'as I have no idea who you are.'

So, with this volume of information being posted, anything I happened to see in my newsfeed was down to pure random chance. Or was it?

I wearily glanced at the post at the top of the page.

'This was my five-year anniversary present from my darling,' it read, with a picture from one of those spoofy Ladybird books about mindfulness.

Sarah, still a Facebook friend, was tagged. The message was from her partner, the one she'd got together with a few months after me. I remembered her telling me about their first date in the spring of 2011. We'd had a sort of 'goodbye' picnic in my garden on a beautiful day, trying our best for a less spiky closure than the abrupt email ending a couple of months earlier had been. We'd pooled together to put on an array of the best cheeses, breads, olives, artichoke hearts, ham and fruit. Yet it had been excruciatingly sad for both of us. She had cried as I told her about my first few dates with Jen. We were both just starting to move on but finding it tough.

I tutted and shut down Facebook. Of all the things I could have seen, this wouldn't have been my first choice. But my brain continued whirring even if I didn't want it to.

Wait a minute. This didn't add up.

It wasn't even a full five years since Sarah's catastrophic email.

There had been an overlap... a month, at least... that snowy pre-Christmas time, after I had stayed over at her place for a couple of weeks. And then, more critically and painfully, the lie was continued for years and years. A more palatable narrative was constructed around a March beginning, when in fact they had already been together four months.

Maybe it had been going on longer in an emotional, if not 'official' sexual, sense. She had stayed out late with 'people from work', the future partner among them, many times over throughout 2009 and 2010. The first time had triggered that awful text row when I was on the train home from a gig in Blackfriars. She had always been defensive about where they were and what time she was coming home.

I'd always known I didn't have the information I needed in order to get over Sarah, recover and move forward. Something *had* been kept from me.

I remembered sitting on the floor in her flat at the time, in shock, asking through burning tears, 'Is there someone else?'

'No,' she had said, defiantly, certainly, calmly.

I should have listened to Liz Bentley. 'There's *always* somebody else, Rosie,' she had said.

'Fuuuuuuck,' I let out a long, sweary sigh, still locked in the same uncomfortable position, half-sitting, half-crouching on the stairs, the rough carpet digging into my bare legs.

Although I felt some sense of liberation and vindication at my prolonged paranoia now taking on a more rational hue, it was a poisoned chalice, a bitter prize. It had taken so long to get to this truth that I had been in limbo for five years, suspended in formaldehyde like one of Damien Hirst's carcasses. Waiting, waiting, waiting... to know the thing I suspected, to have it confirmed.

And *this* was why Anna's behaviour three years earlier at my intimate show in Camden had felt so uncomfortable, so distressing. I *did* know that wall of silence and denial after all. It's just that I had desperately wanted to turn a blind eye to the secrets it concealed. Anna had become conflated with Sarah in my mind. That was why I pursued her confession and repentance so urgently.

I phoned Jen in her lunch hour.

'Sarah was cheating!' I said, without much introduction.

'Oh, well, that *is* interesting,' said Jen.

Her ever-rational tone made the revelation feel like a long-overdue conclusion to a science experiment. A forensic investigation had finally unearthed a buried clue. But it was more than that for me, more emotional.

Now I was free of ambiguity and anger. Now I finally had closure on my last truly romantic relationship, all kinds of new possibilities hovered back into view. Maybe I could be happy again. I could finally break up with my past.

But what did that mean for my relationship with Jen? She was intrinsically wrapped up with my pain.

CHAPTER 3
REBOUND RELATIONSHIPS

'If I could have willed myself to love her I would have. I tried to will myself, in fact, but love doesn't work like that.'

Susan and I were Facebook messaging after she had found herself compelled to break up with the woman who had hoped to rescue her from the fallout of Anna's infidelity. The depressing domino chain of transferred heartache was back in full swing. Like teenagers forced to play a childish game of a forfeit-loaded pass the parcel against our will, we all tried to rid ourselves of the burden of pain as quickly as possible and throw it away. Sadly, the masochistic side of human nature meant that there was pretty much always someone happy to catch it and try to fix everything.

Comedian Sy Thomas performs a very funny routine about taking in a broken bird, a metaphor for a recently-dumped new female partner, making her a lovely comfy bed in his shed, feeding her from a pipette and finally proudly watching her fly and fly and soar... onto another man's penis. It seemed that I had not been alone in finding myself in a committed relationship without having been able to process the previous one. But I had been unusual in sticking out the discomfort for as long as five years. I desperately wanted to stop the dominos from toppling. I wanted to avoid passing on the burden of pain to Jen. So it had stuck to me, an amorphous brown gloop weighing me down.

Questioning the origin of my unbreakable bond to Jen, someone with whom I knew I didn't fit conventionally in either a sexual or romantic sense, I turned to the book *The Chemistry Between Us* by Larry Young and Brian Alexander. In it, they describe some rather sad experiments with prairie voles, a species often used in studies of pair-bonding. They form particularly strong connections with a mate due to a sophisticated system of dense oxytocin receptors. German scientist Oliver Bosch came to Young's lab to investigate what would happen if these adult bonds were interrupted. He placed virgin males with 'roommates' – either a brother or an unfamiliar virgin female. The opposite-sex pairs mated and formed a bond. Then, after five days, he split up half of the brother pairs and half of the male-female pairs before putting them all through a series of behavioural tests.

In one of these, the voles were forced to swim to see if a survival instinct would kick in and they would paddle furiously. This is what the voles who had stayed with partners or brothers, or been separated from brothers, did. Yet the males who had been 'divorced' from their female mate, floated listlessly, not caring if they drowned. (In fact, rodents are mistaken in thinking that they'll drown if they don't manically swim. But for some reason, the instinct remains.) Tragically, the heartbroken males were exhibiting signs of depression, or what Young describes as 'passive-stress coping to deal with the overwhelming anxiety of partner loss'.

I thought of the times I'd spent moping in bed in the bleak days following Sarah's email, listening to Dusty Springfield's 'I Wish I Never Loved You', too lethargic and immobilised by grief to do even the most mundane tasks like feed and dress myself. It was the same type of withdrawal that the poor voles were experiencing.

Interestingly, however, when Bosch investigated the blood chemistry of the vole groups, he found that the still-paired males had similarly high levels of stress-related hormones to the separated ones. Although they were not depressed... yet. He describes this effect thus:

'I compare it to a rifle. As soon as they form a pair-bond, the rifle is loaded with a bullet. But the trigger isn't pulled unless there is a separation.'

The cruel mechanism of animal and human reward systems means that we are, quite literally, ill and injured if our partner is no longer around. Bosch even argues that we sometimes return to a partner we no longer like just to put an end to 'the misery of the separation'.

Bosch primarily studied responses in male voles. However, Young goes on to state that female voles also display depressive behaviour, not only if they've been separated from a bonded mate, but *also* if they lose a mother, sister or close female they've shared a cage with. It was in this sort of state of profound hopeless despair over Sarah that I had first met Jen.

On rebound relationships, Young and Alexander say, 'sex itself is not an addiction... But sex does trigger oxytocin release, which quiets the heightened stress response to separation from a loved one. People who are newly separated from a love relationship, even if they initiated the breakup, can still experience the drive to relieve that stress, leading them into a new pairing.' This sounds like a whole different brain cocktail from the heady one of oxytocin, dopamine *and* opioids we feel for a first love or a new love after a healthy break. Are rebound bonds tying us strongly to someone who doesn't even make us feel good?

I typed another message to Susan, indicating that I understood why we got into these situations even though we often knew deep down that they weren't going to work out.

'It's just too hard to say no when someone is being cool and lovely and you're just still exhausted and confused by the breakup, and you feel like a tree uprooted.'

I once heard Australian comedian Celia Pacquola

describe this predicament even more eloquently, comparing her newly-dumped self to a hose that had suddenly become detached from its hydrant. Flailing around, we leak this chaotic, cascading torrent of love desperate to pour itself all over a new recipient. Often, any recipient who steps in the way of the flood will do.

CHAPTER 4

A DATE!

'The trouble with being in a relationship is that you have to allow yourself to be vulnerable,' said my hot date.

'Yes, but I finally feel like I'm strong enough to really do that,' I replied, smiling with a deep, glowing, unfamiliar confidence. In the days following Facebook's revelation of Sarah's infidelity, my brain had processed the information and set about rewiring itself, making new, optimistic connections. I felt, at last, that I could gaze out to the horizon and see the possibility of being exactly who and what I wanted to be in a relationship. This hopefulness was growing by the second as it dawned on me that I had accidently stumbled upon someone I was sexually attracted to *and* who made me laugh... the double whammy. Just like me, she combined alpha business nous with performance and creativity. If I could get together with someone as awesome as this, then monogamy would become utterly possible... and really rather desirable.

It was another ridiculously mild winter day. We were the sole lunch customers in a sun-soaked Kentish Town pub backyard. It was all just a little too perfect, as if I had orchestrated my own happy ending. I had the proposal for this book out with publishers so probably needed one. When she picked me up in her car, we even joked about being Thelma and Louise, my ultimate fantasy... Um, apart from their particular choice of finale.

I was taking things glacially slowly. Most of her significant relationships had been with men, her sole liaison with a woman lasting a mere few months. I didn't dare ask why. Maybe my old familiar instinct to desire the unavailable was kicking in. Yet she had initiated our flirtation and two meetings.

Ignoring my friend Jac's advice – 'maybe she wants you to behave like a man and make a move' – I hadn't pushed for any physical contact over and above a little hand-holding and the most fleeting micro-snog. But that was enough.

We had an affectionate and innocent farewell at the Tube. She was going away to Cannes on business for a week. I skipped down the escalator, buoyed by a feeling of certainty that something would begin more officially on her return. The story unfolding in my head was quite different from the more realistic, truthful one I'd told Jen.

'There's this comedian I gigged with. And we've met up

a couple of times. Nothing's happened yet but maybe she's interested. I'm not really sure.'

'I thought there was something going on,' Jen said.

'Well, there might not be. We'll see...'

The next day, I sauntered across the park for a bracing swim at the Lido. Just before ten was the perfect time-slot, after the before-work crowd and ahead of any kids and families, the warming sun making the water just about bearable enough not to spend the first few lengths swearing under my breath.

As I wandered past the tennis courts, Richard Hawley's yearning song 'Open Up Your Door' started playing on my iPod. Just as the strings began to swell, I spotted some golden leaves trapped in the wire fence and glinting in the morning brightness. I spontaneously took a photo of them on my phone. They were hardly Wordsworth's daffodils, but there was something about the way they hung there, soon to decay yet still beautiful. They seemed like memories of old love, little trophies to be celebrated not mourned.

Maybe Jen and I had ultimately done the right thing by doing what had initially seemed to be the wrong one. Memories of our good times played like a film in my mind. Weekends in Paris, exploring New York, walking on Hampstead Heath, playing together with her mum's dog Roxy and making her sick with excitement on Christmas morning. We had been way less sexual than either of us would have liked, but we had supported one another intellectually and, as a result, had both flourished professionally. She had been promoted several times over. I had found ways to bolster my stand-up income and profile with articles, radio broadcasts, podcasts and talks. Perhaps sometimes we are supposed to be challenged in a relationship, to be given a reason to think and question who we are, to fit oddly with the narrative we have become so accustomed to. Five years of compromise would be more than worth it if we went on to have decades of friendship.

I felt my pace quicken and launched into a run into the big, open space leading down towards Herne Hill, doing a quick semi-twirl and joyful dance.

I pictured myself onstage performing a new show. That was always a sign that my mental health was back on track. I couldn't quite work out what it would be about yet. But I could feel the energy of it. I wanted to be authentic and mix up the comedy with some poignancy and pathos. One of my favourite fringe theatre venues, The Etcetera in Camden, was inviting applications for a festival. I made a mental note to submit an idea.

I had felt like I was pushing water uphill for years. Yet now I had clarity. Even if this potential fling with the bisexual comedian turned to nothing, I had identified what I was looking *for*. And knowing what you're looking for makes it a hell of a lot easier to find.

CHAPTER 5
A DATE ... FOR HER

2016 was going pretty well. I had a publisher for my book, a new show getting rave reviews and a booking from London's prestigious Southbank Centre. I bypassed the agony and stress of Edinburgh Fringe for the first time in a decade, instead focusing on other festivals and a July adventure at a writer's retreat in Los Angeles.

While I was there, I Facetimed with Jen early every morning to see what she and Lily were up to for what was *their* evening. I felt closer to her than ever. And, for the first time, despite our wildly differing backgrounds, I met a group of people who instinctively understood my ambiguous relationship situation. It was Natalia, a fellow writer in my non-fiction group, who articulated it best for me. Sitting on the steps leading to our accommodation and drinking wine from a mug one humid evening, she said,

'Yeah, I get it, she's your person.'

Meanwhile, non-fiction tutor Sarah Schulman endorsed my conviction that there was something complex and insufficiently documented afoot in lesbian partnerships. 'Writing about romantic relationships between cis women is an endless swamp,' she said in her dry New York deadpan manner, before going on to describe a somewhat bitter older lesbian who once told her, 'half the world has a penis.... and the other half has brain damage.' It was a pretty depressing and outrageous gender-binary statement but I could see how a gay woman could become sick enough of the typically treacherous cycle of heartache to get to that kind of thinking. I was halfway there myself.

Sadly, my reconnection with my 'person' back in London was a little hampered. I succumbed to a nightmare cough almost as soon as I landed, all the excitement of a busy year suddenly taking its toll. I did what I often do when I'm physically ill and retreated into myself. The infection dragged on... and on... and on.

'Go to the doctor's,' said Jen, tetchily.

'Yeah, if it carries on, I will,' I croaked. But somehow I never got around to it.

On hot days, I took my notepad out into the park and half-heartedly worked on the opening chapters of the book. Then one morning I was shocked back into action.

Although Jen had moved downstairs, she still kept all her work clothes hanging in the roomy wardrobe space upstairs.

So I often got to see her wandering around naked, even though it was getting a bit inappropriate.

'Are you away tonight?' she asked.

'No, I've asked Sophia to fill in hosting for me because I'm still not well... Why? Were you planning to have your girlfriend over?'

It was meant as a joke.

She laughed nervously. I sat upright in bed, propping up the pillows. We were about to have a way more serious conversation than I'd anticipated.

'Oh, hang on, you *really* are...?'

'No, but I've got a date tomorrow and I might be staying over.'

It didn't make sense to me. This was big news. But her delivery of it was so casual. How long had she been in contact with this woman if staying over was already on the cards? Was she so easily ready to jump into sleeping with someone else? I wasn't sure how that was possible? I certainly hadn't found it so. Flirtations, fantasies, crushes, a little kiss here and there, yes. But I just hadn't been able to contemplate the realness of being naked with anyone.

If anything I'd been feeling closer and closer to Jen and drawn back in to 'us', whatever that was. But clearly, she had been psychologically moving away from that, readying herself to move on.

Much as I wanted her to have the freedom to explore the parts of herself that she couldn't with me, something felt wrong about the way this was happening. I knew she must have been talking to this woman for a while... in our house, in secret. I had hoped that all our recent discussions had opened up the possibility of us talking about prospective new lovers well in advance.

I had an empty weekend looming, one I'd anticipated spending with Jen as usual, cleaning and tidying the house, playing with Lily, cooking some healthy food to set us both up for the week. It was too late to make lovely, distracting plans with other friends. The only thing in my diary was a press screening of *Manchester by the Sea*, a film I desperately wanted to see but knew would only serve to exacerbate my grief. Kenneth Lornegan's previous work *Margaret* had left me battered for days.

I wondered if my emotional response to Jen's announcement was just plain old jealousy. Was I simply less evolved than my poly friends Kate, James, Dave and Stephanie? I certainly wasn't feeling particularly 'frubbly'. But, more than feeling uncomfortable with the mere act of Jen sleeping with someone, it was what I knew it would *represent* for her that worried me. I realised that deep down she was inherently monogamous and craved to be with one person in a more complete union that ours had been. I wasn't sure any new partnership of hers could co-exist alongside the practical, platonic, family-like, safe, supportive environment we had.

I was in the kitchen, tearful now, following her around

while she got her bag ready for work and wolfed down her breakfast.

'But I need to protect *this*,' I said, gesturing with my hand to the space between us, the house, our home, Lily, our family.

In evolutionary terms, I was 'mate-guarding'. My fight or flight response had kicked in. And I was ready to fight. This new love interest threatened our stability, precisely because neither of us *is* very naturally good at polyamory. And if we were monogamous, it automatically meant losing so much of the precious stuff that we'd built. This was, effectively, Jen breaking up with me.

CHAPTER 6
RECOVERY

'Am I bipolar? A friend at a party asked me if I was.'

'No, that's a misuse of that word. You like to amplify and analyse your ups and downs to explore them in your art. But that's the case for a lot of creatives.'

'Am I a love addict?'

'No.'

I had decided to see a therapist fortnightly. My jealousy and despair at the foundations of Jen and me being so shaken had taken me by surprise. She was away every weekend with her lover. I felt wretched shuffling about the house alone with Lily, who was displaying unsettled, nervy behaviour of her own.

The low point came one Saturday morning as Jen buzzed around the house, excitedly packing her overnight bag. She called out from downstairs. I didn't respond because the name she shouted wasn't mine.

I slammed my door, assuming she must be on the phone to the new woman. I hated her doing that in the house while I was there. A few minutes later, I marched down the stairs.

'Where were you? I was calling you,' she said. 'The big, tabby tomcat came in and was chasing Lily. I was trying to shoo him out.'

'You didn't call me. You didn't use my name. You used her name,' I said, coldly.

'No, I didn't.'

'Yes, you did.'

'Fuck off.'

Jen hardly ever swore at me. We were clearly in a bad place.

'I'm going to hand in my notice with the landlord on Monday if it carries on like this here,' she threatened.

'Christ! You can't do that. This is my home, our home.'

The following week, we talked more calmly. She agreed to keep her name on the tenancy but was going to move out for a while to her mum's, just north of London.

During that shaky and unsettled month, texting and reaching out to old friends was a lifeline. Alice was away on business in the US. We messaged through the night while I was lying awake, shaking and sweating with a feverish anxiety that I might lose my home and family. On her return, we met for a drink for the first time in months and discussed staying close to an 'ex', which now, sadly, felt like a more appropriate term for Jen.

'It's hard when you get a new partner,' she said. 'They have to be very secure to embrace a best-friend-ex.'

Alice was right. New partners were certainly a factor in our own post-relationship connection becoming so much more sporadic. Still, it was great to meet up now and then for a conversation with someone who knew me so well and could make me laugh, even in turbulent times.

'How long do you think I should leave it before *I* go online and start dating again?'

With a typical cheeky glint in her eye, she looked at her watch, paused thoughtfully for a moment and said, 'About an hour?'

The therapy sessions were helping too. I felt seen, able to shed that sense of frustration that I might be talking an alien language that nobody else understood.

'Why are you here?' asked my therapist.

'I think one of the main things is to reconnect with my own sexuality. I feel so shaken by Jen having sex. Not so much because I want to keep her all to myself... but because I feel threatened by *anyone* having sex and enjoying it. I feel like it's a party I'm just not invited to. I'm excluded.'

We talked very directly about my sketchy history with the concept of my own consent and my relationship to my body. We discussed how lesbian relationships, in particular, seem to have very blurry boundaries.

'It's less defined. I see lots of couples who shouldn't have

315

got together. They would be brilliant as friends instead. Straight people don't do that quite so much.'

'Yes!' I nodded, thinking of Jen. 'It's just so, so difficult as gay women because there aren't really any maps or narratives to follow. There are no role models.' Inwardly, I wondered, 'maybe I could be a role model for myself.'

One week, after my appointment, I treated myself to an extensive, pampering haircut in town then bought myself a few new clothes. 'Jen would have a heart attack' I smiled, thinking of her despairing at my scruffy around-the-house uniform of the same old jeans and sweatshirts.

I was starting to feel comfortable in my own skin again. Making an effort to meet up with friends and get a party invite or two had been a great start. I was beginning to embrace the energising freedom of feeling more authentically 'single'. Jen and I exchanged messages about Lily, work and life and occasionally met for lunch. We were getting on and moving on amicably. I felt that it was time to give dating a go and see if I could give myself permission to be sexual again.

Once I put myself out there, it was clear that I had way more choices than I ever realised. Not only in sheer numbers of interested suitors. But, perhaps for the first time in my lifetime, being a single woman was emerging as a more socially acceptable and stigma-free option too. If there wasn't anyone available who was good enough to commit to, then I could wait until there was. I had never felt that before. Feeling in control of my choices transformed the agony and stress that I'd experienced in previous skirmishes with online dating into a joyful experience.

Even though my new lover S was fiercely sexually monogamous, she looked at me over lunch one Saturday and said, 'Why doesn't Jen move back in?'

'You're not supposed to *want* me to live with my ex!' I laughed.

'But you're really happy when you've spent time with her,' she said.

She understood me like no previous partner had seemed to. She could see me emotionally, perhaps because we shared some similar defining life experiences – losing a parent relatively early, being with a closeted partner for years. It was all immensely sexy... and a little unnerving.

I knew Jen wouldn't be coming back to the house, much as I would love it. Her new relationship had faltered, perhaps irrevocably damaged by its unclean start. She wanted any subsequent new partner to see that she was fully available. I understood that, frustrating as it was to be pulled back and limited by the old monogamous rules.

But the important thing was that S was listening to my take on fidelity. I had no problem with a partner whose boundaries were so clearly defined along physical lines. I could be exclusive in that sense, no problem. I craved that, in fact. Yet like many women, straight, gay or bi, I needed a constellation of other *emotional* bonds orbiting around that primary connection. Without them, I would be like a grieving little prairie vole, too stressed-out to function. And there needed to be clear, honest, open communication about all of those bonds.

For me, that was a complete and utter redefinition of what monogamy meant. It was light years away from the secretive, paranoid, lonely, assumption-loaded version of it that I'd experienced. Without these additional, valid avenues for giving and receiving non-sexual love, any central sexual relationship would probably fail and crack under the weight of expectation.

And I recognised right then that S really wanted it to work. She was committed *and* we had a real connection. It had taken me near to three decades of searching, speed-dating, swiping, being set up by friends and trying and working my guts out with slightly incompatible partners... but it was just possible that I could have finally found my chocolate salad.

CHAPTER 7

A MONO STORY:
MY NEW ROLE MODELS

It's no accident that, as I was starting to sort myself out emotionally, I became drawn to the positive energy and outlook of a lesbian couple a decade older than me who lived down the road in Streatham Hill. Perhaps it's too strong to say that Jac and Angie became my 'new role models'. I didn't want to repeat the mistake of investing too much in the success of someone else's relationship, as I had with Anna and Susan. What's more, I remembered how Alice and I often felt burdened when friends said, 'if you guys ever break up, what hope is there for the rest of us?' And, well, we know what happened there. But these new near-neighbours certainly provided an inspiring example of what a healthy and strong female-female partnership could look like. I asked Jac what their story was.

'Angie and I met through an online forum in the year

2000, at forty and forty-one respectively. Both of us had had monogamous relationships which ended because our partners had slept with other people. We were both emotionally devastated, struggling with the fallout in our social groups, all the financial impacts and, in my case, a pre-teen child too.

Mutual practical advice and support soon became a daily email update. We were both very clear about not wanting another relationship in a hurry, but were looking for "laughter and hugs".

In the carving up of resources, my ex-partner got the car. I still had to get my son to school. Without a second thought, Angie let me use hers without any caveats. It was an enormously kind and trusting thing to do. It made me really pay attention because I was used to being the one that took care of everyone. Then along came this person who took care of me.

Through being a London taxi driver, Angie could fit around my precarious timetable. So if I got any free time, she could drop off her last fare and pop round. Cab drivers used to be given free theatre tickets. When I could organise childcare we went to shows together and ate a bag of chips afterwards in the back of her cab parked by the river. We were both broke and this was a really sweet treat: no hassle, no game playing, just simple and straightforward. When I think back on it, those evenings feel like an oasis in a mad, noisy time.

I remember when the tone changed from friendship to romance. I had made some unintentionally ambiguous gesture which Angie sought clarification about, making it known that if I was interested in her, she was interested in me. She sent me an A to Z of things we could do on a forthcoming night out. Most of the options were pizza-film combinations... and a few included the bedroom. I was a bit annoyed because things had been so easy and nice and now I had another thing to think about. But I did laugh out loud at her inventiveness and audacity and concluded that, one way or another, the evening would be a lot of fun. And it was. And yes we did get to the bedroom pretty quickly. No pizza was consumed because we were too late to order one. All that Angie had in the fridge was smoked salmon, champagne and cheesecake. I remember thinking that this was my kind of poverty.

Mornings were our best times together and I would often wake up to music, stuff I knew from my childhood. For a while I thought Angie was musically stuck in the 1950s. But it turned out that her ex had taken all the other CDs. Sometimes I woke up to piano music. I was in awe when I realised it was Angie playing. It was one of those mornings that I said "I love you". I don't even know where it came from and started apologising and explaining that I meant that in the moment, not to read anything into it.

During those early months, we went to a party in Leeds where I met a lot of Angie's friends. They were lovely, interesting people, predominantly gay and lesbian. We stayed in an outrageously-decorated room, all zebra print and diamanté. I have a picture of Angie wearing a princess crown, voluptuously lounging under the pink satin sheets. It was all so joyful and light and it was that weekend that Angie said, "I love you," very faintly and repeatedly. She was asleep at the time. Later I asked if she knew what she'd said. She was very embarrassed and didn't answer.

In a more conscious moment, Angie told me that, although I was a free agent, she wouldn't be interested in seeing me if I slept with other people. That took things awkwardly from "friendship-and-fun" to relationship. I definitely didn't feel ready to think about that but I did wonder if it were possible to meet a more interesting, stable, exciting and sexy person who cared for me in all the right ways.

On the drive back to London, we talked and talked about this amazing shared experience with these fabulous people, savouring every moment. Neither of us mentioned the love thing but it was there in the air.

From there, we dived into a hugely intense, wonderful period where we spent every waking hour plotting how to be together. We've now been married three times – as the law has caught up with love. That's sixteen years of ups and downs so far. Both of us are quite intense, which is good when we are both fixed on the same obsession and not so good when we these are conflicting. Luckily we mostly like the same things. This has led to many successful ventures together, the most recent being filmmaking.

We deal with stress in different ways. I like to be still and quiet while I figure things out, whereas Angie likes to talk. So there have been many times when we have had to sit separately on flights. Most of our rows happen in cars, when I'm driving. When we do those romantic quizzes in magazines, we always find we are completely incompatible. If we are Winnie the Pooh characters, she's Eeyore and I'm Tigger. However, fundamentally, we have the same moral code, politics and ambitions. Being out lesbians attracts some odd and inappropriate questions from unexpected quarters. But we can be sure that any young person questioning their sexuality will seek us out.

Monogamy is an absolute for both of us. Why would anyone want to change something that is already excellent? People never talk about chocolate in this way. It's a given that if its Cadbury's that you like, then Cadbury's never gets boring. Sex changes so much in response to different influences like joy and stress. It's important to make time and space for that. We really aren't going to get up to much in a field these days but a stroll in the countryside or dinner by water... anything that shifts the mood out of the mundane works wonderfully. As we have got older, that familiarity and enjoyment of each other is a bonus. It's lovely when we start flirting with each other and wonderful to start the day in our big bed with soft, warm snuggles.

Friends and gatherings are important to us both. We love hosting visitors to London. Our spare room might be occupied seven or eight times a year with people who are friends of friends who we meet for the first time on our doorstep. We do see some friends separately and have our own friends online too. The people around us are so interesting and varied and we derive a lot of pleasure and support from them.

Most of all though, we thoroughly enjoy time together alone. We both know that things don't last forever and are very conscious of the fragility of life. We have shared some very rough times and had to make brave decisions. The hardest thing is staying conscious of what we are doing and not falling carelessly into damaging patterns of behaviour. That starts with paying attention to yourself and making sure that, when things get busy, it's not your personal time together that suffers.'

CHAPTER 8
JEN, IN HER OWN WORDS

'Look! My favourites don't match up at all with the people who've favourited me.'

Jen was holding up her phone and describing the familiar old lesbian reciprocity paradox I'd struggled with for years. We were having dinner together. It was a sign of how far things had come that I knew I really wanted her to meet someone and be happy, even if that meant using monogamous language and defining clearly as 'friends'. In all honesty, I still found our family-like connection more ambiguous than that. But I didn't want my quest for more adequate, up-to-date relationship language to continue to hinder her search for a fulfilling life.

'Who's that?' I asked, 'She looks okay,' pointing at a slightly less scary photo.

'Nope, not when you read her profile,' Jen sighed.

To distract her from her frustration, I asked if she wanted to speak in her own words in the book. We ordered more drinks and recorded an interview...

How did it feel to have a partner who was publicly speaking and writing about non-monogamy?

'I suppose it's hard to know what the difference is between art and life. As a performer you have the tendency to root a lot of your work in your real life but stretch the reality and fictionalise parts of it too. So I wasn't sure at first if it was an attempt to create a piece of work or to question our relationship. I suppose it was both in the end.

I don't find it a very effective way of communicating about such a delicate and sensitive subject because it is impersonal. It leaves the door wide open for others to peer into your relationship and draw their own conclusions, so people thought we had broken up way before I had realised.

Having said that, I think it is refreshing to debate and talk about monogamy with a partner. I think a lot of parameters are assumed.'

What was your standpoint on monogamy previously?

'I guess I believed it was more serial monogamy, just because we live longer than ever and I don't think you can meet someone and stay with them forever now. Well, it didn't happen to me.

Some people do. They are very lucky, although it can't be

easy. It must take a lot of negotiation, patience and forgiveness.

When I am in a relationship with someone, I would view that as being exclusive unless something has been renegotiated or you have broken up. Like most people, I don't like the idea of cheating on a partner. But if two people have agreed an alternative interpretation of monogamy, then that's different.

I do dream that I will meet someone, settle down and find some stability. The constant cycle of breakups is very difficult, even though meeting someone new and getting to know them is exciting and romantic.

We are too restless as humans and we always think someone better will come along for us. The reality is that they won't. Human relationships are all about forgiveness and understanding.'

Do you remember if you and I ever discussed monogamy at the start of our relationship?

'No, I think it was assumed.'

Did you discuss it in previous relationships?

'No, I don't think I had ever questioned monogamy.'

Have you challenged any of your own ideas during our relationship?

'As I say, I think it is very refreshing to debate it openly

and challenge what we do unquestioningly just because society expects us to do it. However I think I am happier in a relationship than being on my own... and if that involves monogamy, so be it.'

Is there anything at all you would do differently in relationships going forwards?

'Probably have the open conversation about what monogamy means.'

Do you think 'conscious uncoupling', or our attempt at something like it, worked?

'I'm not sure. I think you have to "break up" and make that clean start. I think it is possible to remain good friends in time when the emotions have calmed down. You can't spend good years together and get to know each other intimately and share life with each other without wanting to retain friendship afterwards. It is a shame to throw that away.'

CHAPTER 9

TOWARDS A NEW LANGUAGE

The biggest sticking point for me in working out what was happening in my romantic life had been our lack of language. If we don't have words for a particular type of loving relationship, we can't talk about it and it remains invisible.

Much as we can't learn about modern technology from our parents, we can't learn a big portion of what we need to know about relationships from them either... because between their generation and mine, there has been *so* much change in both those arenas. In much the same way that I have to help my dad work out how to use an iPad, I've had to look to my peers and younger people for help and support as to how to understand twenty-first-century relationships. And the clearest way that they were empowering themselves was by creating their own language to describe new relationship forms.

Here is a recap of some of my favourite phrases, some already mentioned, some new, some already existing, some I've made up and am suggesting. Many terms have overlapping or fluid definitions. But so long as we communicate within our relationships about what we mean in any given situation, these ideas are a great start.

Polyamory – The practice of maintaining multiple, consensual, ethical, honestly-declared loving relationships.

Polysaturated – A fun term used in the poly community to declare that you have reached your limit of partners.

Primary – For those who prefer a hierarchical or structured version of poly, this describes your main relationship. Often it might be someone you share your home with.

Secondary/Tertiary – Additional, generally more casual, partners.

Beloved – Some prefer to use this as a way of distinguishing a primary connection from other 'lovers' rather than using hierarchical language.

Spouse Equivalent – A term that writer Jonathan Franzen uses to describe his partner, to whom he is not married.

Compersion/Frubbly – These both describe a feeling of being turned on by your partner being with someone else. It's a sort of opposite to jealousy. Compersion is used outside of the UK, while Frubbly is more common here.

Metamours – Your partner's partner(s).

Parallel Poly – A relationship structure where metamours don't generally meet one another.

Kitchen-table Poly – A structure where metamours would all sit around the table together and get to know one another in a more 'family'-like arrangement.

Open Relationship – A relationship that is not sexually monogamous. However, often means that the primary couple are emotionally or romantically exclusive and might use a system of rules.

Monogamish – Coined by American columnist Dan Savage to describe committed relationships that still allow some sexual activity with additional casual partners.

Don't Ask Don't Tell – A couple relationship structure where both parties agree to turn a blind eye to the other's additional partnerships or sexual activity.

Relationship Anarchy – A practise in which people are free to engage in any relationships they choose and in which there is not a clear or binary distinction between partner and 'non-partner'.

Love-affair Friendships – A deep, romantic friendship that is non-sexual.

Cuddle Buddy – A platonic cuddle partner.

Logical Family – A term used by the writer Armistead Maupin to describe a chosen, non-biological family.

Solo Poly – A poly practise which prioritises autonomy over couple-centrism.

One Penis Policy – An arrangement where a poly man is

allowed to have multiple female partners, each of whom is allowed to have sex with other women but forbidden to have sex with other men. Apparently there are no real examples of a One Vagina Policy!

Triad – A poly relationship composed of three people. Generally, each of the three is sexually and emotionally involved with the other two.

Pivot – In a 'V' shaped triad relationship, the one person who has two partners.

Serial Monogamy – A relationship pattern in which a person has only one sexual or romantic partner at a time, but has multiple partners in a lifetime.

Relationship Escalator – A proscribed, normative narrative that relationships have to keep moving through a series of recognised stages, with marriage and kids as the ultimate goal.

New Relationship Energy – The high, exciting feeling associated with the beginning of a new relationship.

Breakup Energy – The stress that comes after a long-term relationship ends that can translate into a high, exciting feeling at newfound freedom.

Ghosting – Disappearing without explanation as a way of ending a relationship.

Icing – Putting a relationship on hold and postponing a decision about either staying together or breaking up.

Breadcrumbing – Leading someone on with flirty texts and calls but with no intention of acting on it.

It's a little alarming that the three above terms are all describing new 'bad' behaviours. So I'm finishing off with some more compassionate themes...

Conscious Uncoupling – devised by author and family therapist Katherine Woodward Thomas as a way to have 'an honourable or respectful' separation with 'minimal harm to all involved'.

Post-Romantic – A stage after a long-term relationship ends, but where some emotional intimacy remains.

Decompression Year – A twelve-month, consensually-agreed winding-down period from a long-term relationship.

Date Substitute – When we don't fancy someone but instead match-make them with someone else. This is effectively what happens, rather successfully, in the 1981 film *Gregory's Girl*.

Romantic Footprint – A bit like a carbon footprint, we could reduce ours by behaving more ethically and compassionately in relationships and dating. Apps like Tinder encourage us to reject vast numbers of people, and perhaps forget that they are people at all. Offset the number you reject by helping others to find love.

CHAPTER 10

A WAY FORWARD

Joining in with a four-hundred-strong group singalong of Blur's 'Girls and Boys' on a Sunday morning was an odd thing to be doing on a date. Yet I had taken S along to a relatively new discovery of mine, the non-religious fortnightly London gathering, Sunday Assembly. Set up by comedian Sanderson Jones, the idea is to promote values of compassion, community, creativity and consciousness through getting together for talks, poetry and music. Sunday Assembly feels like a 'logical family', just as my beloved gay community once did. The perfect antidote to a stressful week in front of a laptop or iPhone screen, it has become something of a global phenomenon. Chapters have been set up all around the world.

To date, I had only really found this type of conscious and compassionate thinking within poly groups and forums.

I'm sure it *does* exist elsewhere but I had struggled to discover where. Yet, as I scanned the joyful faces that day, the wider world felt a little less cold and selfish. This was really all I ever wanted... to be somewhere with my partner having simple, harmless fun around other humans. Yet the isolating nuclear idea of monogamous romantic love that had been sold to me had seemed the very antithesis of this.

I have moments when I wish I'd never started writing the show that lead to this book. While it has been liberating and empowering to question how I was going about relationships, it has also been painful and difficult. I probably would never have done it, had I not been a comedian and in search of a thorny issue to investigate and discuss onstage. I needed a topic for an Edinburgh show.

It's been tough to do all this work and come to realise that there's still no right answer. Polyamory works brilliantly for some of my friends. Yet we can all be heartbroken, potentially many more times over if we open ourselves up to multiple relationships. A better-informed version of 'monogamy', taking on board some of the concepts of poly, might work for me. Let's hope so. It's only really through considering and trying on a loosely 'poly' identity that I've found a way to be happily monogamous. The crux of it was in being empowered enough to have a choice.

In my survey, I asked respondents to rate their level of sexual and romantic satisfaction as 'excellent', 'good', 'neither good nor bad', or 'poor' or 'other'. By far the largest group to select 'excellent' were the seven people that had already selected the Holy Grail combo of being in a monogamous relationship, having discussed boundaries and never having had an affair. Whereas those in a monogamous relationship who admitted to an affair tended towards 'good', 'neither good nor bad' or 'poor'.

Qazi agreed that discussion of monogamy is correlated somewhat with greater relationship satisfaction, however warned that, 'one methodological problem with this research is that it's difficult to know if such couples are already better at communicating in general – that is the couple 'pre-selected' to be together via assortative mating, the principle that like attracts like in the first place. So they might already be better matched on their preferences, including preferences for monogamy or non-monogamy.'

It struck me that monogamy can probably only work if both partners are happy – happy to be in the relationship in the first place and happy for it to be exclusive. That might be a fluid thing that needs constant discussion and work.

As the respondents were so overwhelmingly monogamous, my survey wasn't a measure of contentment in poly or open relationships. Though I'm pretty sure if Kate and James had answered, they'd have said 'excellent'.

As one of my writers'-retreat colleagues, Carson, said to me, 'No matter what you do about monogamy, you'll end up on the floor crying at some point.' But if we have that vital conversation about what it means, we will most likely also experience a whole ton of amazing love and happiness.

For many of us, simply changing our thinking and language, without huge behavioural shifts, might be enough to promote wellbeing. If we feel we can choose some form of 'monogamy', it feels like a more appealing option than one about which we never had any choice at all.

Or we may decide to completely abandon traditional notions of fidelity. If we can at least accept that relationships are all unique, it encourages us to communicate and come to our own decisions about what works best for us and our loved ones.

ACKNOWLEDGEMENTS

My special thanks go to my agent Laura Macdougall at Tibor Jones & Associates for her support throughout this journey and to all the team at Accent for their passion for this project – Rebecca, Karen, Kate and Hazel.

I was so lucky to have Qazi on hand with his insights, and to have Kate and James, Jac, Dave, Stephanie and others whose names have been changed, share their personal stories with me.

Special mentions go to 'Jen' for her companionship through this odd, turbulent time and to 'Alice' for being around at the worst of times. Your names have been changed but you know who you are.

Further thanks go to the editors at *Diva*, *New Statesman*, *The List* and *Pride Life* who published articles that formed some of the early ideas around this book, to Giles Edwards for his immense enthusiasm in producing my Radio 4 *Four Thought* piece and to Sarah Schulman, my non-fiction tutor at LAMBDA writers'-retreat, for providing immense inspiration as to how to go about writing non-fiction.

A big shout out to the people who donated to the crowd funder that helped me to get to LAMDA and start writing –

Wendy, Donna, Richard. John, Janet, Richie, Matt, Ali, Stuart, Anny, Amy, Sinead and Vanessa. Also to Lucy O'Brien, Clayton Littlewood and Rachel Holmes for their valuable feedback on the memoir that provided material for the middle sections of this book.

And, finally, with love to my new partner S for not letting this book put you off!

Suggested Further Reading

- Modern Romance – Aziz Ansari & Eric Klinenberg
- Rewriting the Rules – Meg Barker
- What do Women Want – Daniel Bergner
- The Course of Love – Alain de Botton
- Screw the Fairytale – Helen Croydon
- The Ethical Slut – Dossie Easton and Janet W. Hardy
- Our Cheating Hearts – Kate Figes
- No More Silly Love Songs – Anouchka Grose
- The New Rules – Catherine Hakim
- Mating in Captivity – Esther Perel
- The Red Queen – Matt Ridley
- Sex at Dawn – Christopher Ryan and Cacilda Jetha
- Opening Up – Tristan Taormino
- Vagina – Naomi Wolf
- The Chemistry Between Us – Larry Young and Brian Alexander

For more information about **Rosie Wilby**
and other **Accent Press** titles
please visit

www.accentpress.co.uk

ABOUT ROSIE WILBY

Rosie Wilby is an award-winning comedian who has appeared on the likes of BBC Radio 4's Woman's Hour. She has performed at many festivals including Glastonbury, as well as being published in multiple national newspapers. She's currently the co-host of Radio Diva on Resonance FM. *Is Monogamy Dead?* follows her TEDx talk of the same name.

For more information visit:

www.rosiewilby.com

 @rosiewilby

/rosiewilby